Footprints

IN THE SNOW

~ ~ ~ ~ ~ ~ ~ ~ ~ ~

Footprints
IN THE SNOW

~ ~ ~ ~ ~ ~ ~ ~ ~ ~ ~ ~

The Autobiography of a
Chinese Buddhist Monk

Chan Master Sheng Yen

A Peekamoose Book

DOUBLEDAY

New York   London   Toronto   Sydney   Auckland

DOUBLEDAY

PUBLISHED BY DOUBLEDAY

Copyright © 2008 by Chan Master Sheng Yen

All Rights Reserved

Published in the United States by Doubleday,
an imprint of The Doubleday Publishing Group,
a division of Random House, Inc., New York.
www.doubleday.com

DOUBLEDAY is a registered trademark and the DD colophon
is a trademark of Random House, Inc.

Book design by Donna Sinisgalli

Library of Congress Cataloging-in-Publication Data
Sheng Yen, 1930–
Footprints in the snow : an autobiography / Sheng Yen ;
[with Kenneth Wapner]
p. cm.
1. Sheng Yen, 1930– 2. Priests, Buddhist—China—Biography.
I. Wapner, Kenneth. II. Title.
BQ986.E54A3 2008
294.3'297092—dc22
[B]
2008001924

ISBN 978-0-385-51330-2

PRINTED IN THE UNITED STATES OF AMERICA

1 3 5 7 9 10 8 6 4 2

First Edition

What is there to worry about in life?
Just follow the causes and conditions.
Days and months go by like waves.
Time passes like fire in the stone.

—Shide, a Tang dynasty monk

Living in this world is like living in a house on fire.

—*The Lotus Sutra*

Table of Contents

~ ~ ~ ~ ~ ~

1	Shoes of Woven Grass	1
2	The Open Door	6
3	Wolf Mountain	17
4	Going to Heaven	36
5	Rites for the Dead	46
6	A Monk's Education	56
7	Army of the Faithful	65
8	Dropping the Mind	78
9	Free at Last	89
10	"The filial son is produced under the cane"	95
11	Wild Potato Leaves	116
12	Lampooned and Feared	132
13	In the Land of the Rising Sun	139
14	Forays West	145
15	Eating Bitter	151

16 Wandering   162

17 The First Altar   172

18 Chan in the Hills   186

19 Drum Beats Fast   193

20 Full Circle   198

Epilogue   207

Editor's Note   209

Footprints
IN THE SNOW

~ ~ ~ ~ ~ ~ ~ ~ ~ ~

Shoes of Woven Grass

I was born in 1930, the Year of the Horse, on the fourth day of the twelfth lunar month, the youngest of my parents' six children. My mother was forty-two when she gave birth to me, and my father was forty-one. According to my mother, I was an extremely thin infant, not much bigger than a kitten. She said many people thought I looked like a rat. That is why my parents named me Baokang (Stay Healthy).

I was born near Xiaoniang (Young Lady) Harbor, just west of where the Yangzi River empties into the East China Sea. I have no memory of the place because a few months after I came into the world, a flood washed everything away, not just our home but our fields, too. Everything we owned ended up in the middle of the river.

After the flood, we stayed with relatives near Nantong. Then we moved farther upriver, about 150 kilometers from the sea, to a district called Changyinsha directly across from Nantong's harbor. We lived in a three-room thatched hut my father put up on an acre of rented farmland.

Summer days were hot; nights, a cool wind blew in from the river through walls of loosely woven reeds. Snow covered us in the winter; we mud-plastered cracks in the thatch against the cold. When there was money for oil to fill the small stone lamps, wicked with scraps of old cloth, my mother and sisters did needlework, sewing, and spinning. My father and brothers made hemp rope and shoes of woven grass.

We all slept in our clothes in one room on beds that were really just wooden boards on four legs with hay underneath us and cotton quilts on top. We woke to a breakfast of corn or oats. Sometimes there was no money for salt.

My job as the youngest child was to go out into the fields and collect the night waste. I would shovel dog, horse, and donkey dung into a grass basket, slide the shovel through the basket's bamboo handles, and heave the load up onto my shoulder and then set off searching for the next pile of dung. A hook on the shovel's handle held the handle of the basket in place. The night waste, and our own excrement (collected in a large clay jar from our rickety outhouse), fertilized the fields.

My father and brothers were accomplished fishermen, both with nets and by wading into the shallow Yangzi channels and snaring fish by hand. Our house was built on a raised piece of land between two of the river's channels. The Yangzi dominated the landscape. It was huge, deep, and cold. The land was flat under a big sky. Dikes lined the river and the roads were raised. There were no trees except on the riverbanks. All arable land was in crops.

We pumped water from the river to irrigate our fields. A man sat on a bicycle, steadily pedaling, powering a water-wheel with buckets that drew river water into the fields. We tilled the fields with buffalo. They were friends that worked for us, so we didn't see them as food. Our family didn't own a buffalo; we borrowed one.

In addition to collecting dung, I had to gather grass to feed our pigs and goats. We needed to cook the grass for the pigs, but the goats ate it raw. We fed them grass because if we fed them other food we wouldn't have anything to eat. We sold our livestock for oil, sugar, salt, and cloth. It was a rare occasion when we ate meat.

Often, my father and brothers worked for other landowners, far from home. They brought their lunch with them, and pots and pans for cooking in the fields. They would leave our hut in the morning, toting all their tools: short-handled shovels that looked like cricket mallets, sickles, iron hooks to dig up the stems and roots of soybeans, and bamboo baskets for carrying mud. We grew rye, cotton, soybeans, rice, wheat, green vegetables, carrots, gourds, peanuts, and lily bulbs for medicinal oil.

At home, we cooked over a small fire of cotton and soybean stems. Our kitchen countertop was clay-faced brick. Our utensils were chopsticks and rough ceramic bowls from which we shoveled up our gruel three times a day. The bowls were as heavy and thick as stone—if you dropped them they wouldn't break. For lunch and dinner, we added sweet potato sticks and pickled vegetables to our gruel. Salty fermented daikon set off the bland porridge and was a special treat.

We had little, and the work was hard. Yet from my perspective, in my memory, our life was happy. My parents were a perfect couple. I never saw them fight; they never even quarreled. This was mainly because my mother was a very smart, very competent person. All my father had to do was work the fields and provide us with food and money. My mother dominated the family; she ran our lives. My father was grateful. He accepted her strength, and, in return, my mother was loving toward him. Their mutual devotion deeply affected me. Whenever I interact with people, I try to harmonize with them, in the way my father did to my mother. He bent his actions, his thoughts, and his heart to her wisdom and will.

Seven years after we moved to Changyinsha I saw for myself what a flood can do, although it didn't affect us directly because we lived several kilometers from the river. I remember that it rained for over a month. The typhoons came and came and came. The winds rose and rose and kept blowing. The rain was dense and lashing. It would storm for days, the sky would lighten briefly, and then the rains would begin again, waves of rain, soaking everything. After the first week or so, the Yangzi started to rise. It started pulling in the land on its banks, sucking the land into itself, getting fatter and fatter, faster and faster, gobbling up soil and trees. It swelled so much that it broke through the dikes into the fields. We didn't need the bicycle man to irrigate now: our fields were full of fish!

When the typhoons finally stopped and the wind died down, my father took me to see how my second sister's family had fared. Although the flood had spared their house, their land was outside the dike and had disappeared. In places where the water had begun to recede, all that was left of other houses were thatched roofs. Debris floated in the water, half-starved dogs and cats clung to flotsam, and human corpses bobbed in the waves. Their clothes had been stripped off, and they had begun to bloat and rot.

The male corpses floated facedown, their bodies arched like bows with only their backs visible above the water. I thought this was because their stomachs had less fat, but I never found out why. Most of the female corpses floated faceup. Their heads were bent back, their hair was fanned, and their feet hung down below the surface. They also formed bows, but in the opposite direction. The children's corpses were bloated like blowfish, swollen and puffed up with sickly white bellies and leprous gray backs. Ducks scavenged their eyeballs. The rain had stopped, the sun beat down, and waves of stench drifted off the river.

It was such an awful experience. Over the next few weeks I kept waking up in the middle of the night in terror. The fragility of life is frightening—not only to adults, but to children, too. The destruction I witnessed was like what Shakyamuni Buddha realized upon enlightenment: that this world is fragile and constantly in danger. The cycle of birth and death is like an ocean of suffering.

At that time I had absolutely no religious beliefs. But standing over the fetid river, watching the corpses drift by, I had a sudden realization that any of us can die at any time. I knew that if we had lived in that area we would have died, too. Seeing so many corpses, the impermanence of life was driven home to me. Yet I felt that it was a very good thing to be alive. In the midst of all that terror, it was not fear that I felt, but that life is good and that we should cherish it. In the weeks to come, the horror of the corpses faded and was replaced with a kind of acceptance. At a young age, I knew that when death comes there is nothing we can do; we have to accept it.

I have seen much death in my lifetime—war, famine, disease. I am at the end of my life now. One day soon I will die. The lesson of the flood is still with me, and I know that there is no use worrying about death. The important thing is to live fully until the moment when it comes.

2

The Open Door

As a child I was always very weak and sickly. I began to walk at three, and didn't talk until five. I was a horrendously slow learner. There was a pendulum clock on the wall at home. My parents and siblings all tried to teach me how to tell time, but it was beyond me. I remember my puzzlement at this great mystery of telling time, and the unfathomable meaning of the arrows pointing in weird directions like ciphers. I loved watermelon, but at age five I could not say the word "watermelon." I knew only that when we ate watermelon we needed to split them open, so I referred to watermelons as "open." My family was sure that I was going to be an idiot when I grew up.

Because I was so slow, I was given the simpleton's job of caring for our goats. I didn't really know what to do with them, so I would bring them to the stream or another nice place for them to graze and leave them there.

"Where are the goats?" my mother would ask me when I came home.

"The goats wanted to graze and not come back," I would reply, and my parents would have to go fetch the goats themselves. They eventually decided that I should just gather grass for the goats. This also was beyond me: the goats were picky and ate only one type of grass, and I did not know which type to collect. I often came home with a bunch of grass that they wouldn't touch.

I spent much of my time alone. There was no one to play with; my parents and siblings were busy every waking moment. During the day I would go and hide in the wheat fields, especially in places where broad beans were cultivated. Their flowers had a very nice fragrance and the beans were a handy snack. I didn't know there was a boundary between our field and our neighbor's. I have an early memory of lying dreamily on my back on a summer day, under a close canopy of green leaves, the earth warm beneath me, thinking of nothing at all as I lazily broke off beans from their fibrous stalks. Suddenly, a stranger plucked me out of my cozy cocoon and asked in a harsh voice what I thought I was doing. I was terrified. It seemed that I had unwittingly wandered into a neighbor's field. One of my older brothers eventually rescued me. I'll never forget my mother's words as I came into our house and she turned from the stove and faced me.

"Why did you become a thief?" she asked. I hung my head, paralyzed with fear and shame.

When I was little, there were only two rooms in my family's house. The interior walls were made of reeds. The ceiling was also made of reeds and was quite low: an adult could reach up and easily touch it. Bamboo beams held up the reeds in the ceiling; we tied iron wires to them for hanging vegetables. There was a shallow storage loft above the reeds beneath the slightly sloping roof of mud and straw. The central column of the house and the horizontal beams were made of wood, and the pillars on the side of the house were thick bamboo stalks. An adult could easily touch the beam of the ridge of the roof by standing on the dining room table. Every two years we had to replace the walls and roof because of rot. We planted gourds on the rooftop each spring, and they ripened in summer, festooning the house and making it into a living, growing thing.

The bedroom had four beds: one was for my parents and me; the other three were for my older brothers and my older sister. My brothers' beds were not really beds; they were chests for storing clothes and bedding. My sister's bed was made of bamboo slats. The only real bed was the one I slept on with my parents, a wooden bed with four vertical poles at the corners and four rods connecting the poles, over which was draped a mosquito net.

We ate at a simple table. Beside it was the small stove, about two by four feet, which could fit only two pots, one small and one big. Behind the stove was a chimney. On the right side of the chimney wall, about four feet above the floor, was the kitchen-god altar, our home's spiritual center.

In the summer, the house stayed fairly cool under our thick hay roof. I still often miss that kind of hay and reed house, the way it breathed and smelled of the summer fields. It seemed sprung from the earth, a part of the rich land around it that was dominated by river and sky.

My mother made all of our clothes from cotton we grew, which she spun into yarn and wove into cloth. I am still amazed by my mother's competence in being able to grow cotton and turn it into our clothes.

I wore my older brothers' hand-me-downs. By the time they got to me, they were covered with patches made from my father's old clothes. I was small and the clothes I inherited from my older brothers were always too big. I looked like a midget wearing a giant's garments. My mother, much to my chagrin, refused to tailor them for me. I remember one bitter New Year's Day when, as a gift, she gave me yet another ill-fitting shirt.

"Why am I wearing old clothes when everyone else has new clothing?" I complained.

"It's newly mended! It's good enough that it keeps you warm," she replied, ending the conversation.

Cottonseed and vegetable-seed cooking oil were beyond our means, so my sisters and mother collected and crushed woodchips or sesame flowers, which they soaked in water and then filtered for hair oil. My mother never wore makeup, but she did use jasmine-scented frostbite cream for her parched ever-busy hands. When she dressed me, I smelled of jasmine frostbite cream. If her skin was really cracked open and the frostbite cream no longer worked, she patched her wounds with herbs.

It was a fluke that I ended up in school when I was nine years old. A well-read old gentleman who could tell fortunes, knew feng shui, and had a private tutoring school recruited me. He convinced my parents that I should have some education. The school was part of his house, in a room where he placed twenty desks. I had no schoolbag, so I carried a basket with ink, a brush, an ink stone, and paper for writing. But by far the most important item in my schoolboy equipment was a bamboo lunch box.

When I went to school on the first day, I needed to prostrate to the teacher, signifying my respect and willingness to learn from him. The old gentleman taught each student individually, rather than instructing the group as a whole, and he taught me to write. I copied characters such as "Shang Da Ren," "Kong Yue Ji," "Hua San Qian," and "Qi Shi Shi." They are all simple characters that mean: "The greatest man is Confucius;

he taught three thousand students and seventy became gentle-men." I traced and recited these lines. Other students had their lines, and the classroom was filled with the sound of students all reciting different lines at once. The teacher ignored the noise; this cacophony of rote memorization and recitation was what passed for education in the Chinese countryside of my youth. When we couldn't remember our lines, the teacher rapped us on the head with his knuckle. I was always being hit. Often, I remembered my lines, but I was too nervous to recite them. After half a year, I was able to recite *The Book of Three Characters*. But the old gentleman's health began to fail, and he stopped teaching.

An opportunistic young man opened another private school in the area and corralled the old gentleman's students, me included. We studied *The Great Learning*, a Confucian classic. On the way to school, I was often waylaid by other kids and drawn into their games. When the teacher asked why I was late, I would lie, saying that I was needed at home. At lunch, I would lie again and say that I had to go home to help with chores. The truth was that my friends and I had agreed to meet that afternoon. Some days I skipped school completely. I brought my lunchbox from home, went to play with one group of friends, ate lunch, and then met up with more of my chums. Then, one fateful day, I bumped into my mother unexpectedly when I was supposed to be in school.

"It was so difficult to send somebody to school in our family," she said. "I wanted you to succeed and go to heaven, but you squander this opportunity!" She gave me a good beating, but I could tell that she was clearly hurt and disappointed because she was crying. I was crying, too, both from the pain of the beating and shame.

"I don't want to go to school." I said through my tears. "Maybe I won't go back."

It wasn't just that I was a shiftless lad: I didn't want to go back to school because the teacher had given me material that was too difficult for a ten-year-old who had just begun to read. I felt humiliated and defeated, fitfully struggling to grasp a text that was, simply, beyond me.

I went back to work with my brothers, collecting dung in the fields. I followed my nose, which was much easier than reading *The Great Learning*. Finding dog dung was a breeze, but it was more difficult to find cow and goat dung because farmers collected it for themselves. We used dung to fertilize vegetables, wheat, and beans. I also collected wild edible plants. Some of these same plants grow in New York City's Central Park, and I've often thought it's a waste that we don't eat them, especially because they are quite delicious. In addition to collecting animal droppings and wild vegetables, I helped my parents grow rice in summer, wheat in winter, and beans and vegetables in the spring and summer.

In my memory, no matter how much we managed to grow in any given season, there was never enough to eat. This may have been because sugar, salt, and oil were so expensive. The government controlled the trade of these items. Sometimes one hundred catties of wheat bought only two catties of salt. Most of the sugar and salt went to the military. The government allotted a catty of sugar to a woman after she gave birth. If she didn't have milk for her baby, the baby would be fed sugar water.

Toward the end of my tenth year, I encountered my third teacher. He was a doctor of Chinese medicine in his twenties who was our neighbor. Because he didn't have many patients, he started a private school for children. His wife helped, so it was almost as if we had two teachers. At last, I was in a school that was rewarding and fun. Those two young teachers clearly cared about their students, and in the first half-year that I was enrolled, we finished the material for the second grade.

There was one incident that stands out from that period in my life. A girl sat next to me who was a year younger than I. Her family owned a candy store, and each day she brought a roll of fruit candy to school and sneaked it to me. She would not play with the other kids, only with me. But then she became ill and stopped attending school. I don't know if I missed her or her candy more, but in any event I often hoped for her return. When she did return, however, she was blind in one eye. I felt embarrassed, as though she was in some way deformed, and I refused to let her sit next to me. She was hurt and stopped coming to school altogether soon after that. I count my behavior in this instance as one of the worst mistakes of my life. I was consumed by guilt, but no repentance can make up for my actions.

I studied with the doctor for about a year. But war was upon us, and we were caught in battles between the Nationalists and Communists. It was often too dangerous for children to go to school, and the school was eventually closed.

When a battle was going on during classes, we would all hide under the desks, which we covered with blankets. We did the same at home when battles broke out nearby. Gunshots cracked all night. I eventually went back to school with yet another teacher and studied *The Great Learning* again. This time it took. I was motivated and felt that if I didn't study I would not have a future. I memorized *The Doctrine of the Mean*, Confucius'

Analects, and half of Mencius. I still remember those texts word for word.

After attending school for several years, I could do simple bookkeeping. To be able to write a letter required at least three years of school, and where I came from, that would have been really impressive. Teachers were usually the only local people who could write letters, but then again, very few people from the villages on the Yangzi plain west of Shanghai ever left their towns, so few letters were needed.

My oldest brother lived in Shanghai, where he worked in a store boiling water for people to drink, and he also pulled a rickshaw. Twice a year, he sent money home and paid a scribe to write to us, since he was illiterate. Then, when we received the letter, we had to pay a literate person to read it to us. Finally, we hired someone to write to my brother, telling him that we had received the money.

The mail was sent to a rice store in town, rather than directly to our house. Everyone in town bought stamps, sent mail, and received mail through this rice store. We occasionally checked in at the store to see if we had mail. It was exceedingly difficult to communicate over long distance. If the letter was urgent, we burned a corner of the envelope. One of the workers in the rice store would be dispatched to deliver that letter immediately. Of course, the recipient of the letter had to pay for this service. I still often feel that it's quite a feat that we get so much mail each day.

I will not bore you with too many more stories about my early schooling except to say that I did continue on in fits and starts at a new elementary school, which was given the name of our town, "Happy Extra." The school was run by a local landowner, and it took an hour and a half to walk there.

The school required a uniform, which my parents could not

afford. I was allowed to attend anyway. But those of us without uniforms had to stand at the back of the class, and we could not participate in ceremonies.

"Please make a uniform for me," I begged my mother.

"It's Western clothing, made of a particular material," she said. "I can't make it."

"I want money to buy a uniform," I whined.

"We don't have the money. We don't even have enough to buy you shoes."

I usually went to school barefoot. I argued with my parents for a long time, constantly nagging them to get me the uniform. They felt very guilty about their inability to provide. As a little kid, being poor was very painful.

My early training in memorization served me well. I coasted through the school material and was one of the best students in the class. In one memorable incident, several students had failed an exam. They were summoned to the teacher's office one by one to retake it. The teacher asked a question and the student had to answer. I was listening outside the open window where, just inside, the student stood. I would whisper the answer through the open window and in this way the first student passed the exam. I whispered the answers to the second student, but he froze with fear. The teacher discovered what I was doing and punished me by smacking my palm with a ruler.

Although I received an award waiving all the book fees for the fifth and sixth grades, I had to drop out of school even with that assistance because we were so poor. I was needed to help with the work that enabled us to live day to day and season to season, hand to mouth.

When the Japanese soldiers first arrived in our area, my brothers and father saw them killing people with bayonets, and they also heard girls being raped. Even some children were killed. The carnage lasted several weeks; once the Japanese had cowed everyone into submission, the atrocities stopped.

Our innocuous house was on a remote road. When the Japanese soldiers were around, the neighborhood girls, as well as women and girls from town who had been sent to the country-side to escape the predations of the Japanese, took refuge in our home. We gave them our beds because they were wealthy, and we slept on hay on the dining room's mud floor. We didn't know any of them; distant relatives had introduced them to us.

Each day, because it was so crowded inside our house, every-one went outside. One person was always on watch. Whenever she spotted a Japanese soldier, everyone ran inside and huddled together, reciting the names of Guanyin Bodhisattva and Bud-dha. I find it interesting that even at that young age, with no knowledge or particular interest in Buddhism, I noted that once the threat disappeared, they stopped their recitations.

The Japanese soldiers were predictable; they emerged at certain times of day and didn't check small houses like ours. My mother opened our door and took in these girls like a mother hen taking chicks under her wing. I have a vivid memory of her pleasure and pride in the fact that even though we were so poor we could still help people, providing protection, sanctuary, and refuge.

I was desperately afraid of the soldiers, and that fear per-sisted even after I was drafted by the Japanese to perform man-ual labor. The Japanese insisted that our family send somebody, and all the adults were needed in the fields. I built fortifications and caves for hiding from bombs and fences around the soldiers' billets.

At that time I did not have compassion for the enemy. I was just a regular kid, not some kind of living Buddha. It was only after I became a monk that I knew about compassion. As always, it was my mother who set my family's mood during that period. She wasn't overly worried or afraid. Her attitude was that there is always a way and one has to work hard to find it, and now I see that her wisdom molded me, shaping me into the man I would become.

3

Wolf Mountain

My early sense of spirituality was also derived from my mother. She was a member of the local Guanyin Society, twenty to thirty women who met three times a year to chant to Guanyin, the Bodhisattva of Great Compassion, who hears and responds to the cries of all living beings. Most of the women, like my mother, could not read, so they just chanted simple prayers in a melodic drone.

The women wanted me as part of the group because there was a common belief in China that children—pure of mind and unsullied by unwholesome thoughts such as greed—have a clearer connection to the life of the spirit than adults. But I also think that in subtle and unconscious ways my mother wanted me to chant because she was directing me toward a spiritual life.

I'd chant—a scrawny, sticklike kid among the sturdy peasant women in their padded jackets and pants, who laughed at my bumbling attempts to follow along. We met in different women's living rooms by night, our activities lit by an oil lamp, sitting on wooden benches around a rough wood table. In the center of the table was a statue of Guanyin, in front of which we placed offerings of incense, fruit, and candles.

The women's laughter was indulgent and spurred me on. I chanted with great energy. I grew to love chanting and would often chant on my own while doing chores or walking. I don't think it is an accident that later in life, when I became a monk, a core part of my practice involved prostrations to the Bodhisattva of Great Compassion. I believe that it is because of my good karma in previous lives that I started chanting Guanyin's name as a child. This karmic connection with Guanyin continues to this day. It is the foundation of everything I do.

In Chan Buddhism, wisdom and compassion are inseparable. In Chan practice, you cultivate wisdom, which is the absence of self-centeredness. You can only be free from self-centeredness, however, if you have compassion: an awareness of the suffering of all sentient beings. Compassion allows you to give selflessly. If you are selfish, you will not have much compassion—or wisdom! Therefore, wisdom and compassion are inexorably linked; if there is only wisdom, your practice is incomplete.

Not only did I chant to Guanyin, I also dabbled in another religion, tagging along with siblings to meetings of Li Jiao, Li-ism's Principal Teaching sect. Li Jiao is often translated as "the doctrine of order." It is a synthesis of Confucianism, Buddhism, and Daoism with the worship of Guanyin.

Li-ism's founder, Yang Lai-ju, gathered supporters of the Ming government to overthrow the Qing dynasty. High-level officials from the Ming dynasty had been invited to join the Qing dynasty, but they refused. Some became monks or hermits, while others formed underground organizations under the rubric of religion, hoping, secretly, to overthrow the Manchus. This situation continued for several hundred years until the Republic was founded in 1911 and Li-ism came out in the open.

Li-ist meetings occurred in a big lecture hall that could hold several hundred people, which, incidentally, was also the headquarters for the county administration. Lo and behold, a Guanyin statue stood in the main lecture hall. Guanyin was the figurehead for Li-ism, so I never thought of it as a different religion from my mother's Guanyin society, because they both worshipped the Bodhisattva of Great Compassion.

People listened to lectures and chanted Guanyin's name. The atmosphere in the hall was warm. Relationships in the group felt more intimate than even familial ties. The presence of Guanyin's statue made the hall feel like a monastery. Fruit, tea, and meals were served. Meat, smoking, and drinking alcohol were forbidden, and everyone dressed neatly, in his or her good clothes, and behaved in a dignified manner. There were no class distinctions in the group. Everyone was treated with dignity, but once they went back to their daily lives the rich disdained the poor, or, at best, condescended to them. I was too young to understand the lectures. What I did understand was the language of food, and I loved eating there. The meetings soothed and calmed me. But I didn't think that I wanted to belong to the Li-ists when I grew up.

My other formative religious experience came when Buddhist monks and Taoist priests in our village performed wakes or exorcisms. I loved these strange goings-on. How wonderful, I thought, to be a monk helping the deceased move from this world to the next! The ceremonies were beautiful, full of dignity and dark magic.

During wakes, Taoist priests danced with swords and streamers, bending at the waist, inscribing arcs and circles with long sweeping motions of their arms in the flapping sleeves of their robes. They played flutes and pipes and beat drums, creating a whirling, colorful cacophony—high entertainment for us provincial villagers. They squeezed acupressure points on the mentally ill, causing them to writhe and scream—a commotion that meant the evil spirits were vacating the body. Buddhist exorcists recited scriptures so evil spirits would depart. Taoist exorcists drew magical symbols in the dirt with colored chalk and performed dramatic dances with swords to slay the demons; or they extracted the evil spirit with pantomime and great leaps and stuck it in a bottle, where it would remain for thousands of years, unless the bottle broke and the spirit escaped.

I was drawn to these ceremonies. I wanted to be there at the center of the action, exorcising evil spirits, guiding spirits into the nether world, dancing, singing, and chanting. I wanted to be a performer—to make people laugh, to delight the crowd. I suppose that somewhere inside myself I thought that it would be fun to be a monk or priest. But I never thought seriously about it. These thoughts were idle fantasy.

Then one rainy day in the summer of 1943, a neighbor named Dai Hanqing dropped by our house. He had forgotten his umbrella and was drenched. We gave him a rough hemp cloth to wipe the rain off his face and hair. I served him cold roasted-wheat tea from the big ceramic pot, the color of mud, which we made each day. He sat down, appreciatively sipped his tea, made the elaborate pleasantries and inquiries about our family that courtesy required, and then asked me what I wanted to do when I grew up.

I was thirteen, and it was clear that I had come to the end of my schooling. My parents couldn't afford tuition, much less books. I had no idea how to answer Dai Hanqing. My mother, too, seemed at a loss. Finally she said, "There's a family near Wushi that wants him for their son-in-law. They have fields and property. But their daughter can't speak, and he's our last child. I don't think we can give him up. He's a good boy. When he gets older, we still won't have enough money to find him a wife. He just ended up in the wrong family."

"It can't be so bad, can it, Baokang?" Dai looked at me in a curious way. I often played with his son, so I knew him, and he knew me. Our family respected Dai. He often traveled north of the river, and we considered him worldly and wise. He wore his hair short, without a pigtail, which I thought was modern and dashing.

"Oh, no!" I said in that polite way we Chinese have of making light of hardship. I was only half listening anyway; my mind was on the dismal prospect of marrying the mute girl, who was also deaf and couldn't write. "How would the two of you communicate?" my mother had asked me, discussing the match. "And when the children came, you would have to care for them." I was grateful that my mother wasn't going to force me to marry her.

In the arranged marriages common in China at this time, the wife usually came into a husband's home; in exchange, the husband's parents gave a dowry to the bride's family, and paid for the wedding and the newlyweds' bed. In our case, I would have been brought into the girl's family because my family was so poor.

"We may as well send him off to be a monk," said my mother in a joking way to Dai. He seemed oddly struck by the idea.

"Are you really willing to let him become a monk?"

"Why not? Whatever he wants to do is fine." She turned to me and smiled. "Baokang, do you want to be a monk?"

"Of course I do!"

My mother was speechless. Finally, she said, "You're just full of mischief. Anyway, what monastery would take you in?"

"Wolf Mountain (Langshan) is looking for new monks. Is that what you want?" Dai said to me.

"Yes!" I replied without hesitation, although I had no idea what being a monk entailed. My impression of Wolf Mountain from stories I had heard was that it was a place populated by heavenly beings.

Dai, it turned out, was on good terms with the monks at Guangjiao Monastery on Wolf Mountain. He knew they were keen for young blood. He wouldn't have considered sending his own son there, because he had only one son to carry on the family name. Our family, however, had four sons, so he had thought of us. This, in fact, was the purpose of his visit that rainy day!

Dai asked my mother the time and date of my birth to send to Wolf Mountain, where the monks would use this information to ask for Buddha's approval before accepting me. I would later learn that approval consisted of leaving that information in front of a statue of Master Sangha, Wolf Mountain's founder. When six months had elapsed, a prayer was said in front of the statue, asking if the candidate would make a good monk. A process of divination followed. The monastery's abbot shook a bamboo tube. Inside were bamboo sticks with fortunes inscribed on them. There was a hole in the top of the tube, large enough for only one stick to slip through. The tube was turned over, and if the same divining stick came out three times running, the child was accepted. The number on the stick also had to correspond to an auspicious verse in the sutras. With odds like these, it was a wonder that anyone was accepted!

In my own monasteries today, we don't use this method. Those of suitable age who want to become monks or nuns go through a year-long probationary period before shaving their heads. We want to know what drives them to want to join our order. We check their backgrounds. If we find out, for example, that a potential novitiate has committed a crime, we won't accept him. This is not a moral judgment, and it doesn't have anything to do with doubting the aspirant's sincerity or his readiness or aptitude for religious life. But the police could eventually get on to him and that would damage the monastery's reputation. Mentally ill aspirants are also not able to become novitiates. If, however, a monastic becomes deranged while he is part of the order, we will care for him. It happens. We have one such fellow in Taiwan. Some people think he has a really good practice.

My parents thought Dai was joking. They never mentioned Wolf Mountain to me. But I kept waiting for news. Often, while doing my night-soil chores, I'd look off at distant clouds to the north, and I'd think that Wolf Mountain must be behind them. It was the enormous freedom I envisioned that made me hunger to be a monk.

Summer passed, autumn came, and I had just about given up on Mr. Dai. Then one day he returned, fresh from Wolf Mountain.

"Get dressed," he said to me as soon as he was in the door. "You're going to become a monk."

I jumped up, thrilled, ready to leave hearth, home, and my life of toil. But my startled mother wanted to delay my departure. "He needs new clothes," she said to Dai.

"For the time being let him go and see how he likes it," he said, not so easily put off. "Later he can decide if he wants to become a monk or not. The most important thing is to see if he can get used to the life there—and if the old monk likes him. We can talk then about new clothes. The monks on Wolf Mountain are gods of wealth. When they come down from the heights, it's as if they've descended from Money Mountain. You won't have to worry about clothes, or anything else." This silenced my mother. Wolf Mountain was known as a place where the incense never stopped burning and the money rolled in.

Becoming a monk was no honor. Men who could not afford a wife or were outcasts (criminals, revolutionaries, and rebels) would sometimes enter monasteries. Wolf Mountain, however, was a reputable place. The monks there were well educated, and Chinese society places a high value on education. My parents were seduced by the prospect that their son would receive the education at Wolf Mountain that they couldn't afford. Nor could they afford a wife for me—so they agreed.

The next morning my whole family waited for Dai to arrive. I had a brother and a sister who were already married and lived elsewhere, but they came to see me off. A strange atmosphere hung over our home. I was very excited, weaving a beautiful dream of my future life on Wolf Mountain. My mother watched me carefully, registering my excitement.

"You're going off to become a monk. Aren't you at all sad? I've raised you for fourteen years. Don't you think you'll miss me? Don't you mind leaving your mother? Your mother will certainly miss you!" She wiped her tears away. "If only your parents weren't so poor. But what more is there to say?"

My mother wasn't given to crying, and neither was I. But she was hurt that I wasn't as pained as she was, so she cried. Almost against my will, I found myself studying her teary, down-turned face. She was in her early fifties, still vigorous. Her hair was thick and black, full of energy and health, bristling out from under her bonnet like the head of a broom. But her cheeks and forehead were seamed from the hard, frugal life she had endured. How much older would she be when I saw her next? How much closer to the grave? She had given so much of herself to me, and I knew that I would never be able to fully return that love. Then the tears came.

We left my home at 8:00 A.M. on a warm autumn morning that was clear and bright. Puffy white clouds raced across the sky. As we approached the Yangzi, I heard the ferry whistle blow. This wasn't my first trip across the river: we visited relatives on the Yangzi's north side each year. Dai paid the ferry fee out of his own pocket, both to help my family and because he was a sincere lay devotee at Wolf Mountain; he was doing the monastery a good turn by bringing in a potential monk.

The Yangzi was ten kilometers wide—an expanse of choppy, wind-swept water. The ferry was a wooden boat with a threadbare cotton sail and no engine. It could hold up to fifty people, but there were only thirty the day of my journey. Passengers clambered on board from the rickety wooden dock, their clothes tied in bundles, their baskets filled with food. A little girl carried a hen in a cage. An old man with wispy white chin whiskers pulled on a dead pipe, his blue-gray eyes filmed with cataracts. The ferrymen, barefoot, jumped around the rigging like monkeys. Their pants were lashed with twine around their narrow waists. They shouted, whistled, and cast off ropes; one of them pushed us off the dock with a long pole. A commotion erupted on shore: people who had come to see off passengers waved and called good-bye. The sail was hoisted, flapped wildly in the breeze, and billowed, drum-tight as the wind filled it. The skiff shuddered slightly, gave a little heave, and the prow cut into the Yangzi's chop. The smell of water was everywhere. Gulls looped overhead, teetering on the gusts. The wind was in my face and my mother and home were forgotten. I felt a boundless freedom, and the tingling of my own life taking form as the wind propelled the boat and clouds shot across the sky.

The crossing was quick, no more than an hour. We disembarked at Renjia Harbor. The port town loomed beyond the docks, a jumble of low-lying buildings and narrow, dusty streets. Coal-fired buses operated between the harbor and Nantong, but we didn't have any luggage so we decided to walk. We headed south along the river on a raised dirt road that carried carts, old trucks, the occasional soot-streaked bus packed with passengers, the rare and enviable tractors, children with reed swishes who guided bleating goats and sheep. We walked among the endless millions of China, mostly barefoot and dirt poor, carrying their meager bundles, the women with sheaves of firewood and river grass strapped to their backs.

It grew warmer as the morning progressed; Dai and I lapsed into silence. We skirted the city of Nantong—a prosperous, industrial metropolis—heading north. Wolf Mountain rose from the plain, looming before us. It seemed to curl toward the clouds, a fantasy of rock faces, thick forest, and magnificent structures with pagoda roofs tiled in gray slate.

We walked through the main gate toward a big fat smiling Buddha statue of Maitreya. What a huge happy Buddha statue! I thought. But as I walked beyond it and turned back to look, there, back-to-back with Maitreya, was Weituo, a Dharma protector who looks like a general with armor, holding a swordlike club used for breaking bones. My next thought was: "Is there such a fierce-looking bodhisattva as well?"

As we entered through the two doors of the main Buddha hall, I couldn't believe my eyes. The Buddha statue was a hundred times bigger than the one in our house. I craned my neck to see its face. Mr. Dai told me that the dust collected from this Buddha filled twelve buckets a year. (I would return to Wolf Mountain many years later to find that this statue had been destroyed during Mao Zedong's Cultural Revolution and replaced, eventually, by a small replica.)

A novice, about the same age as I, struck a bell, bowing down before the Buddha and chanting, "Homage to Dizang Bodhisattva of Nine Flower Mountain, Teacher of the Underworld." His voice was pure and wonderful, transporting me to another world. And I thought, "This is where I'm going to be living. I am going to be just like that novice."

The young monk hit a huge bronze bell with a wooden mallet. Another monk was bowing down before the Buddha.

"Just watch that monk and copy him," said Dai, trying to teach me to do prostrations. But I wasn't paying attention. For some odd reason I couldn't stop staring at the little circle of shaved hair on the top of the prostrating monk's head. He looked like an actor or medieval Christian monk. I wanted to look like that, too. Sadly, it was not to be. That haircut was only for younger kids. Still, to this day, I dream of having my hair like that.

I thought we had arrived, but Dai said the destination was at the summit of Wolf Mountain. Up we went. The steep, narrow path was lined with stone slabs with quotes from famous writers who had visited the mountain, the work of famous calligraphers, and Buddhist scripture. We passed stone turtles as big as dining room tables, their carapaces incised with memorial inscriptions. An assortment of shrines was set in the lush foliage. There was a shrine to the Daoist god Guangong, the god of money, a shrine to the eye-protecting god, a shrine to the North Star god, who granted long life, and a shrine to the Yangzi River god. People prayed from their homes in the direction of Wolf Mountain, asking favors from Bodhisattva Dasheng, bodhisattva of compassion, Wolf Mountain's protector deity. It was believed that the bodhisattva would instruct other gods to help grant individual requests. When their wish was granted, devotees came to the mountain and installed gods and shrines in gratitude.

Not only were there shrines and inscriptions; the path bustled with food stalls that sold steamed buns filled with savory meat or bean paste, Chinese almond and custard cakes, and ginger candy. Dai bought me a cake, which was a great treat, and we had tea. We passed beggars, many of them blind. They held out gnarled, trembling fingers, palms cupped, invoking the Buddha's name and blessing us. Their dead sockets gazed imploringly at me. Pilgrims with staffs walked the path—thin, disheveled men with ropy arms, the smell of incense clinging to their tattered garments and hair.

Finally we came to the summit. It was cooler there, with bright patches of sun and clouds that almost brushed the mountain's crown. We entered a cavernous Buddha hall, dim with candles, the air thick with incense and centuries of worship and prayer. Another huge Buddha statue dominated the room—golden, glowing, and serene. Incense, kumquats, lichees, apples, and coins were placed at the statue's base. Pilgrims prostrated themselves, pressing their foreheads against the cool stone floor. Monks moved through the room in swishing robes, going about their otherworldly business, overseeing the activity and atmosphere with a kind of abstracted, solemn benevolence.

The theatrical carnival mood of the provincial exorcisms

and wakes, which had so impressed me as a child, was distilled here into a calming, potent elixir. Centuries of lips had kissed the floor. Generations of monks had performed identical ritualistic movements through the hallowed, timeless space. The ceiling high overhead was braced with painted beams, soot-stained from the smoke of the many small pyres of homage, kindled ceaselessly in the halls of Wolf Mountain.

Dai told a monk in fine gray robes that we needed to see the abbot. The monk disappeared into the gloom of the hall, and Dai did his own prostrations before the Buddha. A few minutes later, the monk returned and said the abbot would see us in his room. He then led us down a series of winding paths that dipped and turned through mossy rocks. We passed through gate after gate. The mountain was covered with all kinds of trees, birds darting about in their limbs; half-hidden by the foliage were red walls and gray-tiled roofs of monastery buildings, the corners of the roofs flaring upward like wings.

I'd never seen so many rooms, apartments, magnificent and elegant structures, and I was becoming quite overwhelmed and lost when, finally, we came to a chamber of clamorous monks who all stopped talking as soon as I entered, looking up and measuring me.

"Is this him?" one asked Dai.

"Yes. It's him."

The monk motioned to me. "Come. Let me introduce you. This is the great patriarch, this is the great grand master, this is the grand master, and I'm your master's master. Your master isn't here today."

My master was another novice, a year older than me. We both shared the same room. We would get up in the mornings at 4:00 A.M. and tumble into bed at 10:00 P.M. The monastery life was a blur to me in those first months. I have a vague memory of looking after the vegetables in the garden, taking good care of visitors so that they would donate more money, and making sure that beggars didn't get their hungry hands into our donation box.

We recited sutras and practiced chanting. Only the old masters meditated. They told me I had many karmic obstructions, so I had to perform prostrations to repent. My obstructions, they said, were the reason that I was having so much trouble memorizing the sutras we recited in rituals. I thought it was because I had a bad memory. But after doing prostrations for three and a half months, I had an experience that convinced me they were right and allowed me to fully enter into the life of Wolf Mountain.

Every morning and evening I did five hundred prostrations before Guanyin—the same bodhisattva of compassion to whom I had chanted with my mother. Normally, I found the prostrations difficult and would sweat profusely. But one morning, well into my routine, I felt a force enter through the top of my head, flowing down through my body. The prostrations became effortless and natural. The movements kept happening, but my mind no longer directed my body to do them. I felt cool and refreshed, and my mind became clear and bright. It was as if the bodhisattva had come and given something to me, as if a block that I wasn't even aware of had been removed and a cap had been taken from my head. After that my mind became sharper, my memory was better, and I could learn much faster. Since that experience, I have believed that doing prostrations does help dissolve karmic obstacles. We should realize that in any worthwhile endeavor, there are going to be karmic obstructions. This is why Chan places a great value on perseverance and diligence.

This was my first religious experience. From the perspective of the Buddhism that I practice, I would say that I was tapping into the karma of my previous lives. When one has done spiritual practice in a previous life, you could say that a seed has been planted. In this life, if given the opportunity (through repeated prostrations, for example), the seed sprouts. This was by no means an enlightenment experience. It simply helped awaken my faith.

The old masters took note. They didn't say anything. But I began to understand the deep gleam I saw in their eyes, and the subtle dance of their steps as they moved through the halls in their somber robes took on a new meaning. My eyes were suddenly open, and I began, for the first time in my life, to truly learn.

My master, Langhui ("lang," bright; "hui," wisdom), enlisted two old teachers to help me with my studies. One taught me Confucius and the other taught me about Buddhism. Both teachers were in their sixties and had once been monks but had returned to lay life. From my Buddhist teacher, I learned how to do the morning and evening service and to understand the Dharma content of these rituals. This led me to understand proper Buddhism. Morning and evening services contain Buddhism's main themes. The complete liturgy book is an inch thick, and it takes an hour in the morning and an hour in the evening to go through it.

These liturgies contained the key Buddhist teachings of the Three Jewels, the Buddha, the Dharma, and the Sangha. They also explained the three disciplines of Buddhism.

The first discipline is *upholding the precepts*, which has to do with one's ethical conduct—Buddhism forbids killing, lying, stealing, sexual misconduct, and using alcohol or drugs. The second discipline has to do with *cultivating samadhi*, concentration—training the mind through meditation. The third discipline is *cultivating wisdom*—the proper understanding of karma (the law of cause and effect); of codependent arising (in which all things exist as a result of causes and conditions coming together); of impermanence (that all things experience constant change and therefore lack enduring reality); and that suffering is a pervasive fact of existence. Attaining wisdom means that one has grasped the true nature of the illusory self. These concepts make Buddhism different from theistic religions in that Buddhism locates the causes of suffering and the means of relieving suffering within each of us.

A prominent part of the liturgy also consisted of reciting the great vows, especially the vow to help sentient beings realize the Dharma path. The liturgy also contained passages from the *Amitabha Sutra* on repentance, and the teaching from the *Avatamsaka (Huayan) Sutra* that all Buddhas of the past, present, and future are created in the mind.

All these teachings helped me to overcome the dualistic view of the nature of things. I learned that the world and our minds are not separate, and that the dualistic separation between the self and others is at the root of so much of human suffering and conflict.

If one understood the liturgy, one understood basic Buddhist theory. Most people did not understand the content of the liturgy, but I was very lucky that my master at Langshan hired these tutors for me.

I had been brought up like most Chinese, instilled with a deep sense of the Confucian values of loyalty and responsibility. I was further inculcated at Wolf Mountain by my Confucian tutor with the sense that to become a moral person one had to regulate one's thoughts and behavior and to act with moderation and decorum, to carefully weigh the pros and cons of any action. That was how one became socialized. Confucius also taught that one doesn't live only for oneself. If you're a layperson you have a primary responsibility to your family; if you are a monastic, that responsibility is directed toward your monastery. Confucius urges us to become useful. He teaches a path of interaction with the world that is gentle and subtle and is about cultivating ourselves so that we have beneficent harmonious relations with the people around us. The Confucian sense of responsibility and loyalty would shape my life and fit hand-in-glove with the Buddhism that I absorbed.

Life in the monastery continued quietly until 1945 when the Japanese army surrendered and a battle began between the Nationalist and Communist armies. First, the Fourth Army arrived in the vicinity of Wolf Mountain. Naïve does not begin to describe us monks and the people in the surrounding area—we had no idea that the Fourth Army was Communist. We were so happy when they appeared, assuming that because they were Chinese great fortune had descended upon us after the long and perilous occupation by Japan.

The Communists presented themselves as of the people and for the people. They seemed considerate and kind and conducted themselves well—they didn't demand food or bully people. But then the murders began. Gunshots crackled in the night, and the local gentry and government officials disappeared one by one, found dead each morning, dumped in ditches or floating in the river.

An atmosphere of terror prevailed. People huddled in their homes, afraid to travel. No one came to prostrate in the great

Buddha hall, and the donation box was empty. I did my practice, grew vegetables, and took care of my master and my master's master, Guantong ("Perfect understanding"). I had a persistent cough, which later I would learn was tuberculosis. My sister and sister-in-law would die of the disease, but fortunately, the lesions in my lungs would calcify on their own, without treatment—a fluke, since I had been such a sickly scrawny child. I had had two horrendous bouts with malaria, and I had also nearly killed myself when I fell from a tree that my chums had dared me to climb.

All of my young life, it seemed, was marked by turmoil and upheaval. The Nationalist army came to Wolf Mountain, displacing the Communists and seizing control of the countryside. The Communists went underground and conducted a guerrilla war.

Squads of Nationalist troops encamped in our monastery. Each time a new squad arrived my master would prepare a special dinner for them. But they took it as a matter of course. They moved down the mountain en masse to fight the Communists, who vanished before them like smoke, sniping at them and ambushing them when they least expected it. The Nationalists were soon terrified of the guerrillas and dressed in civilian clothes when they went to town, and they made me accompany them! They were a ragged bunch, equipped with American-made weapons and little else—poorly paid, underfed, and in a perpetually foul mood. They took the ancient monastery doors off their hinges and turned them into beds, broke priceless antique tables and chairs and turned them into firewood, and beat the monks when they protested, me included, although I was spared much corporal punishment because I was still a child.

It was if they were wolves in human form. They tore apart the monastery, and terrorized the countryside. The monastery could no longer support its monks and we left one by one. Eventually, it was my turn to go, and I went to Shanghai, to a temple that was an affiliate of Wolf Mountain. I left the ancient monastery where I had found the meaning and purpose of my life.

4

Going to Heaven

Master Langhui and I left two old monks on Wolf Mountain to look after the place and took a boat down the Yangzi River from Nantong to Shanghai. I was fifteen years old, sad and a little bit nervous to be leaving the ancient monastery that I had come to call home. But I was also still a kid, excited to go to the big city and see the wondrous sights, which I had heard about throughout my childhood.

The trip today between Nantong and Shanghai takes two hours, but at that time it took one to two days. Our transport was a large coal-burning steamboat with a paddle wheel that turned as slowly as a watermill. As we set out, the river was dull and gray, and the low sky was heavy with clouds. The weather turned nasty, and the passengers, myself included, ducked below deck where it was unbearably stuffy. The weather brightened, and we all rushed up to the open air and were showered with coal dust that spewed from the boat's smokestack. I made my way to the bow, leaning forward into the wind that blew the dust away, inhaling the rich wet scent of the river and wondering what was in store for me. China was in tumult. But I viewed the future with a sense of equanimity that had little to do with Buddhism's doctrine of mutability and transience. I had lived through floods, wars, and the hardships of poverty and the feeling that there was never enough to eat. My experience had taught me that life was precarious and precious. I felt part of the great moving mass of humanity uprooted by the great events of a world that was beyond my comprehension. And I was young, filled with the innate optimism of youth. Life was opening before me and I leaned forward to meet it, braced against the wind, eager to see what was coming next.

That night, I preferred to sleep on the deck rather than in the unventilated cabin. I curled up to the wetly percussive *gon, gon, gon* of the wood paddles as they lifted up the river and pushed the boat forward slowly through the mist. I woke to the raucous cries of birds swooping in from the sea, my face black, coated with coal dust.

Shanghai looked like a range of mountains rising up into the gray sky. As we approached the harbor, my eyes widened. I had never seen Western-style houses, and I kept thinking they were mountains; it seemed impossible that such tall structures were man-made.

As my master and I disembarked, travel agents who worked for the hotels clustered around us, grabbing at our luggage. It seemed to me that Shanghai people were so friendly! After all, they had come to meet and welcome us. They even wanted to carry our bags. My master, however, was jittery and commanded me not to take my eyes off our few meager belongings.

A slew of rickshaws (which we called "trolleys from the Eastern Ocean" because they had been imported from Japan) were parked at the pier. My master started bargaining with the drivers.

"Shanghai people like to cheat country bumpkins," he told me. He eventually came to terms with one driver and off we went. I gasped when I saw what I thought were houses that were moving on the road. "Those are buses and trams," my master explained. I couldn't believe what I was seeing! They were light gray and ran on rails. When I got over my initial shock, the scene struck me as quite funny. The trams looked like giant bugs, and the rails were antennas that stuck out from their heads.

"Do people live in those trams?" I asked my master. He laughed at me. I could not conceive that they were used for transport. This was who I was at age fifteen. I was beyond innocent. I had grown up in a world that had been largely unchanged for centuries, and in one fell swoop, I had entered the twentieth century.

I quickly saw that it was a century of noise and haste! People hurried along the streets, looking busy and purposeful. I had no idea where they were going or what their lives might be like. The trolleys clanged and shook. The city buzzed and heaved. The rails screeched; cables crackled and flared. People cried out. The air was filled with commotion and discord, and our meager little rickshaw threaded its way through the tumult, tossed this way and that, the driver crying out against the din.

We passed shopkeepers in stores and stalls, selling things that I'd never seen before. I was very curious. Some stores didn't have merchandise at all, just people. I wondered what these stores were for. My master told me these places were offices, not stores. I asked him how the people there earned money.

"It's complicated," he replied.

Bearded watchmen with turbans wrapped around their heads stood guard in front of the offices and wealthy people's homes. My master told me they were East Indians.

"Shakyamuni Buddha was also Indian," I said. Buddha must have looked like the guards, I thought, excited. I also thought of Bodhidharma. According to the depictions of him, Bodhidharma had long hair, a beard, and big eyes. So I assumed that the watchmen were Buddhist.

"Perhaps we could invite them to teach us Dharma," I said to my master. He looked at me uncomprehendingly. Later, I found out that Indians who wrap their heads in turbans were Sikhs. In fact, very few Indians were Buddhists. But I still felt close to them because they came from the land where the Buddha was born.

I nearly cried out as we approached the thirty-three-story Hotel International, which was the tallest building in Shanghai at that time. "This building is so much taller than the pagoda at Wolf Mountain," I said to my master. People peered out the hotel windows. "Are those people angels or immortals?" I asked. In my hometown, only very rich people could live in houses that were two or three stories tall. I thought since these people lived in such a tall building, they must be extraordinary.

"Mostly foreigners live in the hotel," he explained. "They come from all over the world."

Our arrival in Shanghai had coincided with the end of World War II, and Shanghai, which had long been China's most international city, had many areas that had been leased to foreign countries. The International was in the former British territory, but the British had left China, and the area had been returned to the Chinese. Foreign merchants were still doing business in Shanghai, however, and it was mostly this group who occupied the hotel.

To my mind, the foreigners had magical powers. How had such small people managed to build such a gigantic building?

People waiting to cross the road looked like herds of ducks, all staring at the red light and waiting for it to turn green, then moving like water in a stream. I felt the insignificance of each person. No one noticed us; we were just two people in a huge crowd.

Then I began to feel sorry for our rickshaw driver. He had pulled for over an hour from the pier to the monastery. We had rickshaws in the countryside, but I was aware of how much harder the work was in Shanghai. The driver had to be on constant alert. There was the chaos and commotion of trams, buses, and hurrying crowds through which, shouting and dodging, our driver forged his way. In the future, I avoided taking rickshaws whenever possible. The drivers were so pitiful. If no one took rickshaws, my fellow monks pointed out, then all the drivers would starve. So I did end up occasionally patronizing them.

We left the commercial area of the city and went into what seemed to me like a never-ending labyrinth of narrow alleys flanked by walls and gates. This was a quieter world of hidden courtyards and private lives. Tiled roofs flared beyond the walls, and from the interior of the compounds I could smell charcoal fires and food cooking, and I heard the sound of water splashing against stone. We went over small bridges and across murky canals that smelled of sewage and vegetable rot.

My master and I eventually came to Dasheng Temple, which was located on a narrow lane behind a textile factory in a residential area of ordinary houses. The temple was in a state of expansion and flux. The same pressures that had driven my master and me from Wolf Mountain were causing monks throughout the countryside to abandon their posts and flee. The city generally was filling up with people from all over China who were caught in the crossfire between the Nationalists and Communists.

Dasheng's four buildings faced east. Two dormitories flanked the main hall. The buildings were spartan, musty, and rather utilitarian, with none of the rich atmosphere and palpable tradition of Wolf Mountain. Still, when I saw the Buddha statue on the altar of the main hall and smelled the burning incense my heart soared: I felt as though I had come home. I did my prostrations, and arose with a bittersweet shock. I knew that in the short years I had spent at Wolf Mountain, home for me had become wherever there was an altar; my parents and our house of mud and reeds was a thing of the past.

When the Japanese had occupied Shanghai, an official of the Chinese puppet government who was Buddhist had raised money to construct the large fourth building, but he was executed after the war for treason. The building remained unfinished and empty, except for statues of Cheng Huang and his wife, folk deities.

The statues had come from superstitious people who supported Quiet Calm Monastery, an affiliate branch of Dasheng where I would later pursue Buddhist studies. The monastery was in a quandary; it did not want to dispose of the statues, but it did not want to display them either. So they were sent to Dasheng.

Soon after I arrived at the temple I asked our abbot if these folk "gods" were Buddhist.

"The 'gods' are merely borrowing our place to stay," he replied without batting an eye.

I didn't say anything, but I was taken aback. One could say that the abbot had adopted a pragmatic approach to a problem. Even at my young age, however, and with my limited training and experience, I felt the oddness of his response. Although there is tremendous flexibility and diversity within Buddhism itself, I thought the abbot was being far too accommodating and lax. In retrospect, I think it is fair to say that Dasheng was emblematic of what Buddhism in China had too often become—an accommodating amalgam that had lost sight of its clear principles and purpose.

If I had been the abbot of Dasheng, I would have asked to have these statues removed. Already, I had the feeling that Chinese Buddhism needed to be reformed so it was not mixed with folk religion. The mixing together of Buddhism and folk religion was why people thought Buddhism was merely superstition. At that time, very few people studied or taught the sutras in China; most monastics simply engaged in Buddhist rituals. Even at venerable monasteries such as Wolf Mountain, god statues were everywhere. They were not allowed inside the temple, but were positioned outside on the hillside for people to come and pray for prosperity or health or a more specific request.

As monks poured into Shanghai, they began to occupy the empty building at Dasheng. In front of this building was a well where people came each day to draw water and do laundry. We also drew our drinking water from that well, so it was quite busy each morning. It felt like a place where the neighborhood women came to rub shoulders and gossip rather than a cloister.

Behind Dasheng was a swath of open land where both the temple and the textile factory planted vegetables. Beyond, the city's outskirts resumed haphazardly, small plots of farmland broken up by residential pockets, industrial buildings, and warehouses. You could hear the crickets calling through the night. Mosquitoes swarmed on warm evenings, and in the first false light an hour before dawn when I woke (and have woken for all these years) a cock crowed. China's rural agricultural vastness lapped at the temple's gates, but you still felt within the orbit of the city itself, its heated energy and cosmopolitan culture.

Because of my farming background, one of my jobs was to cultivate crops at Dasheng. And not only did I know how to plant vegetables, I could also grow the most valuable of foods—rice. This was an important skill that was in high demand. The Nationalists occupied Shanghai and the surrounding area, but the city was not entirely safe and peaceful. There was serious inflation, daily life was insecure, and rice could be very difficult to obtain. Merchants hoarded it in their warehouses to create shortages and then made windfall profits by jacking their price; we called them "rice worms."

At Dasheng, we ate rice porridge, and sometimes pancake, fried cruller, or sticky rice with fried cruller rolled inside it and soy milk. This was what we got when times were good. Otherwise, we had rice porridge with fermented tofu and peanuts or pickled cucumber. For lunch we usually had two to three dishes and a soup; rarely did we have four. The dishes were very simple: carrots, green vegetables, and tofu in each dish. Dinner was pretty much the same as lunch. Sometimes we cooked soybeans with soy sauce. We also ate pickled daikon and salted vegetables, which in Shanghai were called "salted chicken."

Life in Shanghai could be intimidating. When I went out shopping, people would hear my country accent and call me "country bumpkin." I understood them because the word in Shanghainese sounded similar in my own dialect. It was difficult to understand much else because not only were they speaking their own dialect, the young people often bandied about English sentences that they had transliterated into Shanghainese.

Western influence was everywhere. There were English signs on shops and most people wore Western clothes, saving traditional

Chinese dress for formal occasions. When I saw women wearing Western-style high heels, I worried for them. The heels were so narrow and tall that I wondered when they would topple over.

People ate bread and milk, foods that did not exist in the countryside. I saw potatoes and tomatoes for the first time. We called potato "Western taro" and tomato "foreign eggplant." I also saw my first foreigners, the British and French who had stayed behind after the war. The Western-leased areas where they lived were always clean and mosquito-free. The Chinese areas stank and were infested with every kind of vermin. I wondered at the difference. Someone explained to me that the Westerners' sewage system drained water very effectively while the Chinese systems were clogged most of the time.

An incident occurred soon after I arrived at Dasheng that made an enormous impression on the neighborhood, which I recount to give you a sense of the temple's spiritual ambiance. At dusk, my fellow monks and I were working the cool soil of the temple's plot when we saw two white foxes picking their way through the fields. At first we thought they were fast white cats; then we saw their distinctive bushy tails, pricked ears, and tapered snouts. They sloped forward, low to the ground, looking this way and that.

Chinese people believe that the white fox is an incarnation of the spirit of an ancient immortal; the fox's white fur indicates its great age. To see even one white fox is rare; two together are extraordinary. People came in droves to Dasheng as word of the foxes spread. One person decided to donate two eggs each day to these incarnate spirits. The eggs were left out at night; each morning we found empty unbroken shells. How had the foxes managed to eat the eggs while leaving the shells intact? The empty eggshells were collected as souvenirs.

A skeptic among our parishioners, who didn't believe that the foxes were immortals, began to refer to them as "stinky foxes," which sent the fox cult into a frenzy. Soon after he publicly uttered those harsh words, he woke one morning to find that his clothes had disappeared from his bedside and had been hung over beams in his house. My master told him that he had insulted the fox immortals and must repent. The day after he repented, the clothes returned to the space next to his bed, neatly folded.

I leave it to you to make what you will of these white fox stories. I was too young at the time, and too fresh from the country, to do much more than wonder and gape. More important, I tell you these stories to give you a sense of the carnival atmosphere at Dasheng. The place was shot through with folk magic, a kind of vague hysteria, and superstition.

Rites for the Dead

My career as a monk took a new turn at Dasheng. Although the temple was nominally Chan, it was not in any way a place for Chan practice, which involves a regular schedule of waking up, eating, meditating, physical work, religious services, and sleep to regulate and calm the mind. Once the mind is stable it is better able to investigate itself and realize its true nature.

Instead, we monks at Dasheng ran around the city like madmen. The temple supported itself by performing funeral rites, and we were constantly traveling to funeral homes or the homes of the deceased. We contracted with three funeral homes in particular. They provided the whole package: a coffin, monks to recite sutras, cremation, and the trip to the cemetery. We were subcontractors and the homes made a commission each time we appeared in our robes and opened our mouths.

It is standard Buddhist belief that there are six realms, of which the human is but one. The funeral rites, which originated in the Ming dynasty, were meant to help the deceased obtain a better rebirth by helping to calm his mind and not letting his greed, hatred, and ignorance guide him to be reborn as an animal or a hungry ghost, or to be reborn in hell. A calm mind might help guide him to be reborn in a more favorable realm, such as a human being, and, better yet, a human being who will encounter the Buddha's teaching. In short, the recitation transferred merit to help the deceased attain better rebirth.

This was an ingrained way of thinking in Chinese culture, which I understand many Westerners find odd. But for most of us Chinese it was just the way things were and what we believed.

Each ceremony required five of us. We often did wakes, keeping the deceased company until four or five o'clock in the morning. Then we went back to Dasheng to sleep for three or four hours before we started the day's work. When the funeral homes were particularly busy, it sometimes seemed we barely slept at all.

We needed the work. If we had business at one place each day, we would make enough money to eat. But we had needs other than food: doctor's visits, building maintenance, and our electric and telephone bills. So we needed to go to three places a day to earn enough to support the monastery.

It was strange. There were high seasons and low seasons for funerals. In high seasons, more people died. In low seasons, fewer people died and there might not be any services to perform for two or three days. Then we would rest. Everyone was starved for sleep and whenever we could we slept right through breakfast.

For me, unfortunately, that was not possible. As a junior monk I had to perform both the morning and evening service. In the evening I was all alone because that service was not required of the old monks. I learned how to use all the instruments in Buddhist services; there is precision and exactitude in how to ring the bell, hit the drum, and strike the wooden fish. I had no training on how to do this because no one else was available to teach me. I had to teach myself, but because there was a need, I naturally picked it up. In the beginning, I hit the instruments in the wrong order, hitting the wooden fish before the bell (yingqing) instead of the other way around, for example, or striking the instruments the wrong number of times, or with too much force or too softly. It took a while, but, slowly, I became more accomplished.

In retrospect it is both amusing and sad that I learned to play all these instruments so that people listening outside the temple thought that many monks were performing the service, actively keeping the tradition alive, instead of just one fledgling novitiate who was often so groggy he could barely stand.

I never saw the other monks study or practice sitting meditation. The temple did not even have a lecture or a Chan hall, the place where, traditionally, monastics lived for extended periods of time, spending their days doing intervals of sitting meditation to cultivate their minds, and eating and sleeping there as well. Not all the temples in China were like that. It was only this way during this particular era in Shanghai. Outside of Shanghai, temples had practice space. During the Second Sino-Japanese War, when many of the temples were constructed, monks attended lectures and sat in meditation. After the war, many monks fled the countryside and these places of practice were ruined. So temples became very complicated places with people with various motivations—dragons and snakes—mixed together.

We worked at large and small funeral homes. The large ones had as many as a dozen rooms of different sizes to rent. The big rooms were pricey and contained musical instruments, such as pianos. In the smaller rooms, people hired musicians from the outside to play the Chinese trumpet. Wealthy people in love with status hired both Chinese and Western bands. They also hired Buddhist monks, Daoist priests, and nuns to do recitations. It was just for show, to make it appear that many people were there to recite for the deceased. Actually, Chinese people didn't really have a certain religious faith per se. They just wanted to cover all the bases, and the ceremonies were rooted in folk customs, with little religious spirit.

Some funeral homes had coffin storage rooms, with corpses inside thick wooden boxes that were sealed tight so they wouldn't smell and piled four high on shelves like cars in parking lots in the United States. Coffins were stored while a burial place was prepared for them, or waited to be shipped back to the deceased's hometown. Some were homeless, with no place to go. In those cases, the funeral home functioned as a cemetery.

People also hired us to memorialize a family member's birthday, the first- or third-year death anniversary, or the forty-ninth day (seven times seven) after the relative had died (although this day was mostly observed only by the very wealthy).

If the family's home was cramped or they had a large number of relatives and friends, services would be held at Dasheng. Strange things occurred during these services, although they may not strike those who have not lived most of their life in a monastery as all that strange. Many of our lay followers ate meat, and, for these ceremonies, they would hire a caterer to cook chicken, fish, and duck at the temple. They also served alcohol, and after these ceremonies Dasheng would reek with the smell of cooked meat. I found this unsettling, to say the least, and I asked the abbot why we allowed meat and alcohol in the temple.

"We let them do their ceremonies here and eat meat, so that we can have vegetarian food to eat," he replied. "If we don't let them do their ceremonies, we will starve. The money we make from recitations isn't enough to support us. So we are just making a living."

After this happened a number of times, I began to want to leave Dasheng. If the temple could be hired out to cook meat to memorialize people, I knew that we weren't truly engaged in Buddhism. Our senior monks did not seem to grasp, let alone embody, Buddhism's basic principles. Even at my young age, with my minimal training and the way that I had fallen into being a monk, almost as if by default, I had quickly and irrevocably become deeply pious. It wasn't a choice; it was just who I was. There was nothing in my approach to Buddhism or being a monk that had to do with "making a living."

Because so many monastics were pouring into Shanghai, the competition for reciting sutras for the dead became quite stiff. We had to find ways to remain competitive by cutting our price and expanding the area we served. We rushed and raced, tumbling like maniacs through the narrow streets of the endless city, our robes flying, our bodies covered in sweat, panting and weaving, dodging bicycles and rickshaws, trying not to knock people over, running as much as forty kilometers each day. We worked hard, slept little, and were constantly fatigued.

There were lots of young, energetic monks who dealt with the exhaustion by injecting or inhaling heroin. These monks had mostly come from large monasteries and many of them were outstanding—smart, knowledgeable in Buddhism, and fluent in Buddhist ceremonial ritual. Also, none of them were ugly: they all looked rather auspicious . . . which was odd, now that I think of it.

Most of these monks had left their monasteries because they were bored. They were young guns for hire. Perhaps other monasteries would hire them as abbots, they thought. It was as if employees from a large corporation had decided to try their luck elsewhere. Although these monks were accomplished, larger monasteries were wary of them because they were transients. So they ended up in small temples like Dasheng and turned lazy. They didn't meditate, read sutras, or do prostrations, and many of them had gravitated toward Shanghai to reap the benefits of the lucrative trade in death rituals.

Heroin helped sustain their energy. But it was a vicious circle: they needed to take on increasing amounts of work to support their habit; and the more they worked, the more they relied on drugs. They smoked heroin by putting the powder on the thin metallic lining of cigarette boxes and burning an incense stick under the lining, sucking in the drug with a straw made from a rolled up piece of paper. They weren't worried that others would see them. Whenever they felt weak, they started using.

The more serious users injected the drug, putting a bit of heroin into a little water (they didn't use distilled water, just regular water) mixed in a teacup. When the heroin powder dissolved, they drew the liquid into a syringe, rolled up their sleeve, and used one of the holes that they already had in their arms for the injection. As the heroin entered their veins, they hissed, feeling really wonderful. Before using the heroin, they had snot all over and were exhausted. But once they injected the drug, they became strong and awake and could do anything.

When there were no rituals to perform, these monks went to prostitutes on Fourth Avenue, one of Shanghai's main red-light districts. Once, on my way to perform a death ceremony at night, I passed by this road. I didn't know why there were so many women there. The prostitutes were very interested in us monks and kept asking if we would like to go home with them. We thought they wanted us to perform the death ritual for them and told them that we were too busy. When we got back to the temple, the more worldly monks asked us if we knew who these women were and laughed at our naïveté. Good thing I didn't take up their offer. I really didn't know that they were prostitutes. They were beautifully dressed, and I had no idea who they were.

Around this time, my father sold some wheat, risking hunger for our family, and hired a tailor to make several sets of monastic robes in our hometown, which my father brought himself to Shanghai. I had never gone through the official head-shaving ceremony at Wolf Mountain and wore lay clothes even while performing funeral rites for Dasheng. Because my family lacked money, all the ceremonies usually associated with becoming a monk had been waived. A monk's lay family has to pay for all the expenses incurred by his ordination—monastic robes and the banquet for the teachers who officiated at the ceremony. I was pleased with my new robes and moved by my family's sacrifice.

One day a group of policemen came to Dasheng to look for heroin, and, of course, they found it. In fact, the temple had become a warehouse for drugs. News of this spread, which was very bad for Buddhism generally and a disaster for our temple. People avoided hiring us for reciting sutras and our income plummeted. But after a few months, people began to forget this incident and hire us again.

Some of you may wonder why the abbot hadn't done anything about the rampant use of drugs at Dasheng. Always the pragmatist, he didn't want the monks to leave because they provided us with income.

I look back on those days at Dasheng as being some of the most chaotic of my life. There was no schedule. Monks were coming and going at all hours. There was no set time for meals. But there was no dissension or contention in the temple. Drugs were our worst problem. We were still vegetarian and, aside from the few bad apples in our midst, celibate.

Then it became even harder to live. Stalls were set up in the streets, manned by former monks who did not uphold the precepts and had been forced to leave their monasteries. They had wives and children and wore ordinary clothes. They were also in the business of reciting sutras for the dead, and they undercut our price. When they conducted a service, they would don their old robes.

Because each service required five monks, these street stalls pulled together to form a sort of union. Each time they got business they could easily mobilize several dozen "monks," and the government and Buddhist associations turned a blind eye to this practice. The lapsed monks were burying us. But if we were too busy and didn't have enough monks for a service, we would hire these "monks," too. So we competed against each other, but we also cooperated.

Eventually I began to think about the choices that lay ahead of me in the monastic life. If I stayed in one monastery, it would support me in my old age. Monks who worked their way up to management or administrative positions were given private rooms when they were old, along with other privileges: they did not have to follow the monastery's daily schedule, and they were attended to by a doctor when they became ill. An abbot was en-

titled to live in a former abbot's room, even after his term ex-
pired, until he died, with a personal attendant and a stipend.
Other monasteries, however, recruited former abbots, and there
were distinguished monks who were abbots at more than ten
monasteries in a lifetime, and were able to choose where they
wanted to grow old and die.

These were the best-case scenarios to which a young monk
like myself might look forward. If I wandered from monastery to
monastery, it was clear to me that no one would provide me with
security or ensure my livelihood, and I would have trouble if I became sick and when I grew old. I saw that there was a safety net,
however. If a monk begged to stay at a monastery, they had to
take him in.

At its peak there were more than twenty monks at Dasheng.
Our core group of monks from Wolf Mountain knew only how to
recite sutras and conduct rituals. Other monks had all sorts of
skills: some could sing opera, perform theater, or play the flute.
Several could play two trumpets simultaneously. Some could play
two trumpets by mouth and another by closing off one nostril
and blowing through the other. They could do kung fu and use
various weapons. When we performed funeral masses, during
the intermission we added these performances, and these monks
could make lanterns, flags, and banners with thick colored paper
to adorn the room for the services.

Dasheng's abbot urged me to learn to play the flute and
trumpet so that I, too, would be able to perform. But I had always had low lung capacity and thus was unable to play instruments that required breath. This turned out to be for the best.
Deep inside me I knew (although I would have had trouble ar-
ticulating this at the time) that I wanted a different life, one that
was about learning and study and the transmission of the
Dharma. These two paths of practice and scholarship were inter-

twined for me, and if I had succeeded on an instrument, I would have become an entertainer and been relegated to that kind of middling life and limited career, and I would not have been allowed to go study and take part in the intellectual life of Buddhism later on.

6

A Monk's Education

Although my temple desperately needed the income from the ceremonies I performed, in 1947 Master Langhui let me enroll in Quiet Calm Monastery (Jingan Si), a Buddhist academy in Shanghai. It was a great thrill for me to attend school again, and this time a school in which Buddhism was actually taught!

Quiet Calm was a completely different environment from Dasheng. We sat in assigned chairs in a classroom with two students at each desk. Because of my myopia, I generally was assigned a seat in the front row. The seat and desks were low, and my neck would ache by the end of the day from constantly squinting at what I was writing and then looking up to squint at the blackboard and our teachers.

There was a piano at Quiet Calm; we learned Buddhist songs with an outside music teacher. We didn't have a library, but the classroom had bookshelves in a corner, stocked with three nationally distributed Chinese Buddhist magazines and a few very good literary periodicals.

It was odd that there were so few books. We were told to focus on our own homework, and not to read outside our own sphere of study. We didn't even have a decent Buddhist dictionary.

The classroom had very good natural light coming in from three sides. A few of the students were bored, they had graduated from other institutes and knew the material that we were learning inside out. While the teacher lectured, they read. Our teachers, as you can imagine, didn't respond well to these students, but we liked them because they were able to help us with our work. When I graduated, several of these students tore up their diplomas because they said they were useless. They already had several diplomas from other institutes and had been unable to get teaching jobs.

We studied important works in Chinese Buddhism, such as the *Sutra of Complete Enlightenment* and the *Awakening of Mahayana Faith*, and doctrinal texts on Yogacara, Madhyamika, Huayan, and Tiantai, which are discourses on the Buddha's teaching and contain the central ideas of impermanence and suffering. The liturgy I had learned at Wolf Mountain was like a basic course in Buddhism, the areas of study that I needed to learn in order to be able to call myself a solid student of Buddhism and carry myself as such. It had taught me that the monks at Dasheng were not acting as monks should. My classes at the institute were something else. These were teachings on theory of mind. They were written by profound philosophers with a very deep understanding of Buddhism that illuminated the true nature of Buddha's words and ideas. This was university-level study of Buddhism.

The seminary was founded by the group led by Master Taixu, one of the great revivers of modern Chinese Buddhism. The effort Taixu put into establishing institutes of Buddhist education was amazing. He started them all over China. This emphasis on the importance of education in Buddhism would stay with me my whole life. The principal of the Quiet Calm Monastery had studied in Japan at the University of Tall Wild Mountain. He had opened the institute for the public in 1945, after the Second Sino-Japanese War.

I glimpsed the Dharma's vast complexity and depth, and I began to understand the ancient lineages and the long traditions that were behind the practices and atmosphere of Wolf Mountain. I don't want to give you the impression that Quiet Calm was a hotbed of intellectual discovery and debate. We learned by the traditional Chinese method—by rote. We were not encouraged to think critically or analyze ideas. We memorized each school of thought on its own terms. We took the same approach to sutra studies. Our teachers believed that we only needed to learn by rote, and with time we would understand. And they were right. I memorized a great deal of material, and as I became better educated, I was able to begin to think about what I had learned and understand it in creative ways on my own.

But that wasn't at all the case at first. I had trouble understanding what was going on. I tried to follow what my teachers were saying by their tone of voice and facial expression, and I was able to guess some of what they meant. I copied the notes from the board and discussed them with my classmates, some of whom understood the material because they had attended other Buddhist institutes. The discussion helped me understand the notes, and I did well in the texts and examinations, scoring at least 90 percent most of the time. So although I entered the institute behind everyone else, I graduated among the top in my class and was among the few who were selected to attend a graduate institute.

As well as Buddhism and Buddhist morality and precepts, we studied English, mathematics, and classical Chinese with lay high school teachers and university professors. The seminary also emphasized physical exercise. We learned Taijichuan and Shaolin boxing with a teacher from the renowned Shaolin monastery.

Our practice at Quiet Calm emphasized ritual repentance. We meditated, but did not have a very clear idea of the correct method of sitting, so it was difficult to gain any real strength from our practice. I was aware that there were people around me who had had deep meditation experiences or been certified as enlightened. They never explained or described their experience. When they talked among themselves, their language was strange, its meaning elusive.

I questioned a few of the older students who had spent several years in meditation halls. When I asked them about meditating, they would say, "Oh, it's easy. Just sit there. Once your legs stop hurting, it's fine."

Sometimes a monk would be given a koan on which to meditate, but on the whole, there was no systematic meditation training.

Once, I participated in a Chan retreat at Quiet Calm. I sat in meditation until I heard the incense board signaling walking meditation. No one told me what to do or gave me any instruction. We had a saying that one had to sit "until the bottom falls out of the barrel of pitch."

Sometimes, while I was sitting, I thought, "What should I be doing? Should I be reciting Buddha's name? Should I be doing something else? What really is meditation?" I kept asking myself these questions, until I became a big ball of doubt. I was plagued by that doubt for years. It was a pressure on my heart and created waves of turbulence and discomfort, even anguish, inside me.

Unfortunately, my education was once again interrupted as my teachers and fellow monks nervously prepared for the invasion of antireligious Maoists. My family were proletariat tenant farmers (without their own farm) so I was not afraid of the Communists, whose officers would sometimes visit our monastery. They were friendly and showed an interest in Buddhism, inviting us to look at what they were doing and how they lived. They said that the country was corrupt and backward under Nationalist rule and as long as the Nationalists were in charge, we, as a nation, would remain listless and depressed.

Several of my classmates joined them, were brainwashed, and returned to Quiet Calm to try to brainwash the rest of us. Later on, these classmates became Communist underground workers when the Maoists entered Shanghai. The Nationalists arrested some of them and they were shot.

I listened to what the Communists were saying, but I suspected their thinking was materialistic. I secretly read books on Marxism and materialism and felt that this ideology was not in accordance with Buddhism. I could have been arrested if the Nationalists discovered this. I also heard that in areas occupied by Communists, Buddhism was under siege and monastics were being urged to leave the monastery to return to lay life to participate in economic production and military. Although the Nationalists were corrupt, one of their leaders, General Jiang Jieshi (also known as Chiang Kai-shek), was Christian and did not oppose Buddhism. My fellow monks and I knew that Jiang's mother was a devout Buddhist, so we believed the Nationalists would not destroy Buddhism.

Some of my classmates joined the Communists because their confidence in the Buddhadharma was not firm. They left home because their families were poor, and they had few opportunities to go to school. They had been tempted by the opportunity to get at least some education, albeit Buddhist, in a monastery, which was better than no education at all.

The Communists finally invaded Shanghai in late May 1949. I remember that the border of the city was lined with stacked-up sandbags, supposedly to defend the city, but it was just for show. When the Communists arrived, there was no battle. They just entered and took the city.

No one was surprised. We were sure the Communists would succeed in invading Shanghai, because the Nationalists had no confidence that they could defend the city, although they had vowed to. We were certain that it was just a matter of time before we would all have to return to lay life. It was tragic and we felt hopeless.

"What are you going to do?" I remember asking a good friend of mine, a monk from Wushi in Jiangsu. "Are you going to return to your hometown? Are you going to return to lay life?"

"My sister lives in Shanghai," he replied. "She has found a girlfriend for me and found me a job." He seemed excited about his prospects.

"What are you going to do?" I asked another one of my classmates, who was from Yangzhou.

"My family has two freight boats that just arrived in Shanghai," he replied. "They gave me laypeople's clothes, and I will be able to do manual labor on the boats."

Another classmate said, "You go join the Nationalist army and I will join the Communist army, and we will meet in the future on the battlefield."

Still another classmate confessed: "I don't have much courage. I don't want to go back to my hometown, and I am afraid to go join the military. So I am going to stay here and see what happens."

In the second half of 1948 and early 1949, there were some monks who left for Hong Kong, Canton, or Taiwan by plane; their masters had money and took them along. They left secretly, slipping away in the night, and we only discovered their escape once they were gone.

When I asked my grand master if I should try to escape, he said, "Even old monks are not afraid, what is this young monk afraid of?" My master was also opposed to leaving the mainland. But Master Shoucheng, the dean of students at Quiet Calm Monastery who was already in Taiwan, wrote me and asked if I wanted to join him. He told me to send him several photos so that he could apply for a Taiwanese entry permit for me. He did not have money or connections in Taiwan and was unable to offer much help. I, of course, had no money, either. The boat fare to Taiwan from Shanghai was ten to twenty silver dollars, and my stipend each month was less than one silver dollar.

Another opportunity presented itself. Sun Liren, a famous general during the Second Sino-Japanese War, who was based in Taiwan, was recruiting officers from the mainland for his corps. Sun Liren had enormous prestige. He was a graduate of a U.S. military academy, and during the Second World War, when the Chinese and American militaries joined forces, he had defeated the Japanese in a decisive battle in Burma.

Sun was accepting educated young people into his training camp, which was located in Taiwan in Gaoxiong. We monks at Quiet Calm received a letter from Tianning Monastery in Changzhou, inviting us to join Sun's corps of young officers.

One of my classmates encountered a recruiter from the communication corps of the Nationalist army. He decided to join them, and his military identification entitled him to free bus fare. When he told us about that, we were extremely impressed, and two other classmates and I went straight to a recruitment station and enlisted in the communication corps. We asked if we were joining Sun's army, and were assured that was the case, and we didn't find out until we arrived in Taiwan that our company, number 207, had at one time been led by Sun, but that he had been reassigned.

The army paid our way to Taiwan. I brought only very simple luggage with me. I carried about twenty books on Buddhism, a blanket, some changes of undershirts, and an identity card. That was all. In Shanghai, I had bought a uniform, and I wore it and put away my monk's clothes.

At that time, my eldest brother lived in Shanghai, where he had been tending a little stand that sold boiled water. When I left the mainland, his boiled-water business had gone under and he had switched to selling soy milk. He was just scraping by. I went to tell him that I was going to join the army, still in my monk's clothes. I didn't tell him my reasons. He bought me a bowl of soy milk and fretted over me, but was unable to offer any help because he was so poor.

When I went to see my brother, I had packed a wooden box with books, photos, essays, manuscripts, and clothes. I asked him to bring it back home or leave it in Shanghai so that when we succeeded in taking back the mainland he could return it to me.

When I returned to the mainland in 1988, I asked my brother if he still had the box. He hung his head and told me he had lost it. He had been on the move almost constantly after the Communists took over, and he had left it somewhere. All my childhood pictures were in it. Such a shame, but that is the nature of impermanence.

When I left Shanghai in late May of 1949, several classmates saw me off. Dasheng was still a temple. I heard in later years that the monastics there had been forced to return to lay life, including my master and my grand master. The young monks married and the old ones just died off.

When I returned to Shanghai in 1988, I learned that Dasheng had become a factory during the Cultural Revolution. It was impossible to imagine making it into a temple again. All statues were destroyed during the Cultural Revolution in 1976.

When things opened up in 1978, people were needed to operate the monasteries. Former monks ran the temples as a day job, returning to their families in the evening. My grand master, who was in his fifties when he left monastic life, had married and had children.

So it was that I left Shanghai and the mainland, a young monk and aspiring scholar who had traded in his robes for a military uniform. It wasn't an easy choice, but I had been backed into a corner. I made a vow a few hours before I joined the army: I would preserve the dignity of my country and people and fight for the honor of Buddhism in decline. My goal was not to remain a soldier. At that time, I thought the Nationalists would be victorious in three years. I had no idea what was in store for me as I made that long sea crossing south and east in that tumultuous spring of 1949 when China was in the throes of revolution.

7

Army of the Faithful

Taiwan is a mountainous island about two hundred kilometers off the coast of southeastern China. A narrow plain runs down its western side where most of the people live and most of the island's industry is located. When I started training as a private in May 1949, Taiwan was nothing like the developed highly industrial island you see today. The island had been under Japanese occupation from 1895 to 1945. When Japan surrendered to the Allies after its loss in World War II, Taiwan was returned to China. In 1949, after the loss of the civil war to Mao, Chiang Kai-shek moved his government and army to Taiwan. In all, over one million Chinese left the mainland for the island. They were mostly the wealthy Nationalist government party members, and soldiers like me.

My life had changed dramatically yet again: how far I was from my village and my thatched roof hut! Gone were the incense-cloudy halls of Wolf Mountain and the mists and flaring roofs and ancient rhythms. The teeming streets of Shanghai were also behind me, and the exhausting life at Dasheng, which, although fraught with compromise, was still roughly Buddhist. I was a soldier now—all myopic, sickly, scrawny 110 pounds of me—and I had no idea what was next.

We trained in the foothills on the edge of the steeply rising mountains in northern Taiwan. The head of our unit drilled into us that in Napoleon's dictionary the word "difficult" did not exist, and we worked to overcome every difficulty without complaint. We built our barracks and mess by hand, using grass for the roofs and walls and bamboo for the pillars, beams, and beds. There were no trees, so we planted them. When we traveled, we slept under bridges, on roadsides, and in the cemeteries.

The army was destitute. We didn't have uniforms, and in the summer we usually wore only a pair of shorts. We called our training sessions the "movement of three nakeds"—naked head, naked legs and feet, and naked upper body. We were exposed to the sun and the rain and became really dark, as if we were from Africa: you could see only our white teeth. When it rained, it was shower time. Because we got so much sun, the water rolled off our bodies as if our skins were waterproof plastic sheets.

We had no shoes, which was hard on our feet when we traveled on rough terrain. We wove shoes from grass and plants that grew along the riverbank. Each pair of shoes lasted about two weeks. Some soldiers weren't skillful enough to weave the grass and put the shoes together, so I told them that if they gathered and prepared the materials I would make the shoes for them. They were grateful and wanted to give me thank-you gifts. They asked me what I wanted. "I don't drink and I don't eat meat. What is there to buy?" I said. They bought me roasted and salted peanuts, a real treat that was usually reserved for captains and lieutenants.

Necessities were scarce. Each group of ten soldiers had only one basin. We used it for everything: a soup bowl at mealtime, a bowl for washing our faces, and to hold mud when we were working on our building projects. Once a group of high school girls came to sing and dance for the soldiers. One had to go to the toilet, but there was nowhere for her to go. We didn't have a fixed toilet ourselves; we just dug a hole when we needed to go. We didn't want her to have to do that, so one soldier held up a sheet for privacy and let her pee in a pot we used for cooking! People said it wasn't a problem because the girl was really clean. Afterward, we took the pot to a stream and cleaned it out so we could use it for soup at our next meal.

No one except our lieutenant owned a watch and there were no clocks on the wall. We would hear the military trumpet call, telling us when to get up, when to eat, and when to sleep. We ran five kilometers in the dark each morning before the sun came up. When we came back, we rested and then trained on gymnastics equipment: the horse, the single beam, the double beams, and a bamboo post that we had to climb up with two hands.

Around nine in the morning, by the time we ate our first meal, we were exhausted. We sat on the ground in a circle around a bowl of water with salt and a few vegetables. We shared that bowl of "soup" and ate rice, our main food. The rice was rationed. We only got twenty-seven taels, less than one kilogram per day. That may sound like a lot but it is only enough for two meals, not three, and our diet was completely lacking in protein. Our second meal was at four in the afternoon. When we needed more food, we would exchange rice for dried sliced sweet potatoes, which were cheaper. The sweet potatoes were very fibrous, without much taste, and they made us fart.

Because we had no protein or other nutrients, we suffered from malnutrition. After I was in the military for two years, we started receiving American aid, which helped. The United States provided flour, soybeans, and medical supplies. We were able to add soy milk and one steamed bun, the size of a small fist, to our breakfast. We also received vitamin pills from the government. Every soldier got a bottle with eighty pills in it. We were supposed to take three a day. But one soldier said, "It's such a problem to take three a day. Let's just take them all at once." Several people did that, and guess what happened? They got intestinal fever and were rushed to the hospital to have their guts flushed out. After that, the captain distributed three pills a day to each soldier and reminded us to take them one at a time.

We spent part of every day in political education classes. After class, we practiced marching. We formed various lines, horizontal, single file, by threes, or one long line. We thought it was silly to train like this since we probably wouldn't be so organized in battle. But the training turned us into a cohesive unit. Our entire corps of more than a hundred people had only two rifles, which didn't even fire, but they did have bayonets attached to the tips. We took turns carrying the two rifles and pretending to be guards. The rest of the group pretended bamboo sticks were rifles and carried them around when we marched.

In our political education classes we learned military strategy and anticommunist theory. These were important classes because they helped change our thinking. When the Communists did that, we called it brainwashing. But we learned their techniques and used them to engage in what we called the "war of thoughts."

From our perspective, the Communists were evil. Our instructor emphasized patriotism and taught that the Communist teachings of Marx, Lenin, Stalin, and Mao were foreign, not Chinese. We studied a book of speeches by General Jiang and discussed them together once or twice a week. We also learned to embrace the ideology of Dr. Sun Yat-Sen, who had set forth the Three People's Principles: one, that the Chinese government should be ruled by the Chinese; two, that the government should be democratically elected; and three, that land ownership should be equalized and wealth more evenly distributed. Dr. Sun said nationalism should provide daily essentials—clothing, food, housing, transportation, entertainment, and education— to people who need them.

"People in Communist China live in communes," our instructors said. "They must wear every piece of clothing for nine years. Three years when it's new, three when it's old, and three years after mending every seam."

We were quite thoroughly brainwashed. We didn't get much information outside our training. We had little contact with locals; their dialect was incomprehensible to us and they considered the Nationalist army an outside occupying force. The Nationalists only published one newspaper, just two pages long, and the military had its own newspaper. We didn't think much about the lack of freedom of speech: we all thought the same way. There were very few foreign newspapers available. We heard just a little news from the outside world, about the problems in the Middle East and the war in Cyprus. We learned about Poland resisting the rule of the Soviet Union. We all thought the same thing would happen in mainland China. We called the Soviet Union "the Iron Curtain" and mainland China "the Bamboo Curtain" because we didn't think it was as strong as the Soviet Union.

We had one day off each week from classes and training. We were tired all the time. But I tried to find ways to maintain my monk's practice. I recited the name of Bodhisattva Guanyin whenever I was doing simple things, like running, marching, or standing guard. There was no time to do sitting meditation or prostrations.

I wanted to enter the officers' academy. I wanted to have more time to practice and read. But because I had not attended high school and didn't have a rounded education I failed the exams many times. My height was five feet eight inches, but my weight was as low as ninety-nine pounds. The moment they weighed me, I was disqualified.

Eventually, I received training to advance one level higher than a regular foot soldier. The biggest problem was my myopia, but I had not had a pair of glasses since I joined the army. Shooting practice was an important part of training, and I could only see the white outer part of the target, not the circles inside, so I only hit outside the target. After an entire day of practice, my score was zero. The officers thought that I had missed the target on purpose; as punishment, I had to do push-ups for every step I took on the way back from the shooting range to the barracks. The distance was 1,000 meters, so I had to do about 1,000 push-ups.

I told the officer who supervised the push-ups that I had myopia and didn't miss the target intentionally. He took pity on me and reported my condition to the head officer. He decided that I couldn't stay in the infantry with myopia, because I would be useless on the battlefield. I was transferred to the signal corps, which was responsible for telephone and wireless communications and where my poor eyesight would not be a handicap.

The responsibility of the signal corps was to guard the coastline. We lived on the windy sands, with the forested mountains looming up behind us, in corroded buildings that were being eaten away by the salt from the sea and constant dampness. We spent our days vainly trying to intercept radio transmissions from the mainland that would warn us of the attack that our superiors assured us was imminent.

It was a blessing to no longer have to march from one place to another, and to have more time to myself. When I was not on duty, I would find a private place on the beach by the water or in the woods to do sitting meditation. I also read as much as I could. At this time, it was impossible to find Buddhist books or sutras. Temples rarely contained sutras, only books of liturgy, which contained mantras, key passages from the sutras, and the great vows and refuges to the Three Jewels and prayers that monastics recite in morning and evening services. Each monastery usually had its own liturgy with content the community deemed essential.

Sutras, on the other hand, are Buddhist scriptures that record Buddha's teachings. There are many sutras, and they constitute religious texts for all Buddhists. The few temples that had sutras would not lend them to me because they were precious. So I found other books—literature, philosophy, and natural science. I read deep into the night, by the light of a lamp that I had made from an ink bottle filled with oil and a piece of cloth. When an officer discovered me reading, he punished me by making me do more push-ups.

I lived among soldiers, but I was always a monk in my dreams and longed to return to the monastic life. I would even tell people that I was a monk. The soldiers spent their leisure time at the movies, drinking, and going to prostitutes. I didn't join them, and while they looked for entertainment I often became the designated watchman of our camp.

I considered all my fellow soldiers friends. We ate, lived, and worked together and got along. But it could be painful living with them. They were constantly doing things and eating things that I didn't feel were appropriate. A fellow soldier, who was Cantonese, once killed a dog and brought it back for us.

"Why did you kill the dog?" I asked.

"To eat," he replied. "We don't have enough food."

The dog meat lasted several days. Instead of buying other groceries, the soldiers spent our food money on salt and seasoning to cook the dog. I didn't have anything to eat; they took pity on me and let me eat rice with soy sauce, without the dog meat.

At another point, we were stationed at an ad hoc army post that had a fish pond on its grounds. Each day I would go to the pond to gaze at the fish, entranced by their loveliness, they way they languidly and effortlessly glided through the water, their fins wavering, inscribing graceful arcs, their demeanor so gentle and tranquil. It pained me when a group of my fellow soldiers, my friends, jumped into the pond and caught the fish, which they then cooked as food for our meals.

Vegetarianism was, and is, important to me because of my monastic vows. Even when I was in the army, I tried to uphold the monastic precepts in my behavior and mind. Chinese Buddhist monastics are strict vegetarians because eating meat is not compassionate. Food is for nourishing the body so that we can cultivate the Path. Since it is possible to nourish the body with vegetarian food, why is it necessary to eat meat, which involves killing animals, especially when one of the five basic precepts taken by all Buddhists, lay and monastic, is not to kill?

It was often a struggle to persuade the chefs to cook something for me before they cooked a meal with meat in it. Some chefs were nice enough to do that, some weren't. I tried not to eat the meat dishes they cooked. But sometimes when they cooked a dish with pork, I would eat the vegetable in the dish and avoid the pork. When the chefs rationed the meat to one piece per person, everybody wanted to be friends with me. They would say, "Monk, if you give me your piece of meat, I'll give you my vegetables."

I was sometimes bullied. Soldiers love to push each other around. The treasurer in our company, who was responsible for distributing our monthly salary, was like that. I asked him to keep my salary for me because I didn't need to spend it right away. He was happy to oblige and said he could even give me interest. But, after several months, when I asked him for some of the money he dug in his heels.

"It's not time for your monthly salary," he said.

"But you've kept my salary for the last three months for me," I replied.

"I'm only responsible for the public fund," he said, "not your personal money. I don't have it."

It was clear that he was bullying me. I let him keep my money and learned my lesson. From then on, whenever something involves money, I have made sure that there is a receipt.

Soon after this incident, the treasurer was stabbed three times by another soldier with whom he had a disagreement over money. The treasurer ended up in the army hospital, and the culprit was sent to jail.

I made it a point never to lose my temper. This was not just because after I entered the monastic life, I had renounced violence. When I was in elementary school, I was in fights all the time, and I lost every one. When people poked fun at me in the army, I tried to tolerate them. I knew that I should not lose my temper. But I also dared not.

I was also a coward when it came to breaking free from the army and returning to a monk's life, the life for which I yearned. I didn't try to escape, although I once considered accompanying a classmate from Shanghai who was planning to run away. I was too afraid. I knew that if we got caught, we would be badly beaten. My classmate knew that I still had the monk's clothing that I'd worn in Shanghai. He asked me to give it to him, which I did, and he escaped that night. So my monk's clothes served some function at least, helping someone else return to monastic life.

My classmate had a better chance of escaping than I did because he still had his identity card from Shanghai. On the boat to Taiwan, an officer encouraged us to give him our identity cards and told us we would get them back when we docked in Taiwan. I gave him my card, but he never gave back any of the IDs. He told us they were worthless and we would get new ones. My classmate, however, knew some foul scheme was afoot. "I was about to join the army," he told the officer. "What was the use of an ID? I didn't get one." But he actually had the card in his pocket.

IDs were issued by government on the mainland. When the Japanese ruled China, the IDs were called "fine people certificates," meaning that this was an okay, ordinary person. When the Communist insurrection began, the Nationalist army would likewise check IDs. In Taiwan, they were also used as means of identification. I was naïve and gave the officer my ID card, thinking that there would be no use for it since I was going into the military. But most of those people who kept their cards escaped from the army to become ordinary people. If I had been sharper, I could have kept the card and would not have had to stay in the army. With an ID card, I could have gone to work as an ordinary person. Without it, I would have been considered an exile or outsider, a suspect person in China's close-knit society.

Being a Chinese soldier in Taiwan in the 1950s was perilous. While the Nationalist government was in power, Taiwan went through its own McCarthy era, trying to root out Communists from its midst. I was wrongly accused of being a Communist three times, and it was only through good fortune that I was not killed.

When I first came to Taiwan, a number of soldiers in my unit had dubious backgrounds. Their accents marked them as people from the Shanghai-Zhejiang area, a hotbed of Communist activity, and they were tight-lipped about what they did in China. People began to suspect that they might be Communists. Because I was one of more than a dozen people from Shanghai in my unit, they investigated me.

The investigators asked me if I was Shanghainese. "No," I answered. "I am from Jiangsu." They told me to be careful.

The others from Shanghai suffered cruel punishments. The investigators tortured them by shocking them with live telephone lines until they confessed their background. One was indeed a Communist. One was shot. Because I was from Shanghai as well, I was forced to watch the execution.

The second time I was accused of being a Communist was after the end of the Korean War. Chinese Communist POWs in Korea were sent to Taiwan by the United States to join the Nationalist army. These POWs were dispersed to different battalions. They all had tattoos that said: "Fight against the Chinese Communist and the Russians. Kill Mao Zedong." They had these tattoos made when the Americans captured them so that they could join the Nationalist army in Taiwan. This started a movement by soldiers throughout the entire army to get the same tattoos as a sign of loyalty. An officer came to me and asked if I had the tattoo.

"Fighting against the Communists is done in the heart, not by tattooing," I said. "I hate the Communists, too. But I won't put tattoos on my body."

"Why not?" he challenged me. "Maybe your resolve is not strong. Maybe you are a Communist."

They began to watch me, and their suspicions put me in grave danger. But I refused to be tattooed. I still planned to return to monastic life, and it's not good to have a tattoo on a monk's body. Because I refused, many others did not get tattooed, either.

The third time I was almost killed grew out of my interest in ancient Chinese poetry. I had borrowed books from the library and copied the verses I liked. One of the poems read as follows:

How wonderful is the wine in this precious glass.
I would like to empty it all while racing on horseback.
Please don't laugh at me lying drunk on the battlefield.
How many have returned from battles since antiquity?

Because I had copied this verse I was accused of being antiwar, and it was suspected that I was planning to organize others to be antiwar as well. I told my superiors that I just thought that the poem was nice, and I often copied poems. This did not make a dent in the suspicious way they looked at me and their biting accusatory tone.

I was in serious trouble. I was watched at all times, and I was not allowed to do anything alone. My case was reported to officers high up in the chain of command, and because they didn't know me it was very possible that they could have ordered my execution.

I was fortunate to be friends with an influential captain who had been a college student in China. We often discussed history, literature, and Buddhism. He supported me by telling his superiors that I was just a monk who liked literature and poems, and that I would not cause problems. He explained that although I might be a little pessimistic about wars because I was a monk, I was definitely not a Communist.

And so I was spared once again.

8

Dropping the Mind

The military life began to drain me terribly, and again I began to think about escaping. I was *ku men*, meaning depressed and low. I didn't know what was going to happen to me or whether I would ever be able to live as a monk again. I had volunteered to serve in the army for life to avoid being conscripted into a combat position. But I figured that when the Nationalists took back the mainland, I would become a monk again. It was clear to me after several years in the army that that was never going to happen.

The simmering conflict between the Nationalists and Communists dragged on and on. General Jiang (Chiang Kai-shek) had told us that it would take one year to prepare to attack mainland China, another year to conduct the attack, and a third to take back the country. But as the fourth and fifth years passed, it became obvious to us that we were not returning to China any time soon. And General Jiang stopped saying we would. The Nationalist government lacked weapons and military personnel. It was not clear whether we could survive a real fight against the mainland, and the Communist government was constantly saying it was going to wash Taiwan in blood. No one's mind was at peace, wondering how long it would be before war would start and how it would happen. Everyone was living in fear, and I wondered whether this life, which was so far from who I was and what I wanted, would be my lot until I died or was killed.

I began to think again of escape, but I no longer had my monastic robes, and I lacked the courage to flee. I saw a person who tried to escape three times. After the first attempt, he was caned on his buttocks so severely that it left open wounds. After the second attempt, he was tied to a post under the sun for two days, without food and water, and left there to urinate and defecate in the open. After the third attempt, he was shot.

Although I felt trapped, as an officer I had time to begin to write essays for Buddhist magazines. Until 1956, I had mostly written literature: poems, short stories, and novels. I didn't really write on Buddhist topics. Nobody paid much attention to my work. But that spring, a classmate of mine from the institute in Shanghai suggested that I change direction, and I began writing essays on philosophy and religion.

My Christian supervisor gave me a Bible. I read it over the course of two months and made notes. He also gave me some books by Christians criticizing Buddhism. I read a book by a Buddhist master that compared Buddhism and Christianity, as well the response to this book by a priest in Hong Kong. I wrote a response to the priest's book and that's what got me started. I read volumes of Western philosophy and books by contemporary Chinese thinkers and began to submit articles to Buddhist magazines that were about the meaning of life and the nature of impermanence, suffering, and loneliness. I advocated that we work diligently to transcend samsara, the cycle of birth and death through which we transmigrate, lifetime after lifetime, until we can eliminate all vestiges of attachment and karma.

I also investigated the relationship between religion and literature, and looked at how Buddhist texts had influenced literary texts. I argued that Buddhists should have more respect for literature than they did, and that literary creations could have a large impact on society and consciousness and were valuable.

I began submitting these essays to Buddhist magazines and they were enthusiastically received by editors and published. When I had joined the military, I had had to give up my monastic name adopted at Wolf Mountain—Shi Changjin—and I took a lay name. I used my family name, Zhang, but picked a name of my own choosing instead of using Baokang: Caiwei ("cai," picking; "wei," rose).

There was a temple on a hilltop not far from our camp. I could see the temple's huge Buddha statue, and I began to do prostrations to that statue. No one bothered me; there were many Christians in the army, and they often attended services.

I also had time for sitting meditation. I meditated on an upper bunk in the bedroom that I shared with several people. My colleagues knew that I was meditating, and they didn't disturb me. I sat in a half-lotus posture. In the army, I wasn't allowed to burn incense to a Buddha statue, so when I sat, I just sat. There was no mattress on my bed. It was just a wooden platform. But because I was an officer, I had my comforter. I meditated for as long as I could, but, because of my job, there was no fixed duration or time of the day for my practice. Sometimes I sat for an hour or two. I could only sit for short periods without being interrupted by people coming in and out of the room and breaking the stillness.

Officers had travel privileges, and I vacationed at monasteries. Taiwanese Buddhism was in transition and there were very few monastics on the island. Japan had left its imprint after fifty years of occupation and Buddhism in Taiwan was mainly in the Japanese style. When the Japanese left, the priests were all sent back to Japan and the monasteries were taken care of by laypeople. There were only religious ceremonies. There were no Buddhist institutes for learning, outreach to spread the Dharma, or teaching of Buddhist practice. The monastery leaders, only some of whom had received monastic training, mainly performed folk rituals and ceremonies for the dead.

The situation, however, was beginning to change. When I arrived in Taiwan, there were probably about twenty to thirty real monastics. Around forty or fifty more came later from the mainland, fleeing from the Communists. Some of them ended up returning to lay life because they could not speak the local Taiwanese dialect and it was difficult for them to spread the Dharma. After the government required Taiwanese people to learn Mandarin, it was discovered that the monastics from China were all outstanding. A number of my former teachers made it to Taiwan and stayed: Nanting, Daoyuan, Baisheng, and Miaoren.

Master Nanting was in touch and cared about me most, often sending me food because he knew that I didn't have much to eat in the army and suffered from malnutrition. Once he gave me condensed milk, an expensive delicacy. I mixed the milk with boiling water to melt it and stirred it into my rice. It was really tasty and smelled good. My fellow soldiers were envious, saying that I must be royalty to drink condensed milk.

Master Nanting wrote often to encourage me. I remember writing to him at one point to tell him how depressed I was. I complained that the army life lacked freedom. In his response Master Nanting wrote: "Who has freedom in this world? As long as there is the body, there is no freedom." He encouraged me to use my body to observe my responses to the environment, to apply my body as a tool for practice. He wrote: "Being a sentient being living in this world is like living in a house on fire, but when Buddha lives in this world, it is a Buddha land for delivering sentient beings. Treat the people in the army as learned friends and maintain your practice; that's why Buddha remained in this world even after his liberation, to help sentient beings." This letter was very useful, and I still have it.

On one of my vacations I took a bus to visit Master Nanting in Taipei. He was living in Shandao Temple (Temple of the Wholesome Guidance), a Japanese temple managed by a layperson. The temple's manager had invited him to live there, but he was not the abbot. He lectured on the sutras once a week, and only a few dozen disciples attended. His living quarters were decrepit and cramped. Because he was a very famous abbot and master on the mainland, a number of refugees supported him, including powerful politicians and generals. Although he had some money, he didn't have anyone to take care of him. He had to do everything himself. When he wanted to write me, he had to travel far to purchase stationery and stamps. Nonetheless, his situation was the object of envy for many monks who had fled from the Communists. He had a place to live, food to eat, and disciples who provided support. Other monks were homeless, wandering through the country with no place to live.

When I visited Master Nanting's, his place was so small, with only enough room for him, that I had to stand. Nanting encouraged me and would give me a five- or ten-dollar note when I left, a lot of money in those days for a poor soldier.

I spent time with other teachers as well. I visited Master Baisheng at Shi Pu (Ten and Ordinary) Monastery in Taipei. He was very busy with his temple and could not talk with me much. He always asked: "Do you have problems or difficulties? Let me know and I will take care of them for you." I also went to Master Miaoren's small place in the countryside. He cooked meals for us, since no one was there to cook for him, and was approachable, charismatic, and encouraging.

Occasionally I stayed at Shandao Temple, the largest monastery in Taipei at the time. It was the Taiwan headquarters for the Japanese Pure Land tradition, a faith-oriented school of Buddhism. The main hall resembled monasteries in Kyoto. But the living quarters next to the main hall were cramped, and I slept in a room that was used to store the urns that held the ashes of deceased Japanese who had been affiliated with the temple during the occupation.

Back on the base, I continued to wrestle with frustration, doubt, and the desire to leave the military. As the years passed, Mao Zedong's power only strengthened in China. We began to hear the saying, "When Mao coughs, the entire world trembles." The population in Taiwan was seven million, and the mainland was approaching one billion; it was hard to imagine how we could prevail.

Most of my fellow monastic classmates who had joined the army had escaped to become monks again. But they weren't very happy monks because Taiwanese society was unstable. People were spreading rumors that the monks from the mainland were spies. The Nationalist government jailed many of them, and those who were not jailed were on the run, disguising themselves in laypeople's clothing and hiding in private homes. They didn't dare stay in monasteries.

I still didn't have the guts to escape, preferring the army to jail. Life in Taiwan was becoming Orwellian. You could be arrested at any time for any reason. There were frequent shutdowns. No court permits were needed for search and seizure. So

I stayed in the army, feeling *ku men* and doubting I would ever be a monk again.

Then I met Master Lingyuan Hongmiao (1902–1988), and my life changed.

We met while I was visiting a new temple in Gaoxiong, called the Gaoxiong Buddhist Hall. Lingyuan was visiting from Jilong, where he lived (and where he was later given a piece of land to build a monastery). It is common for monastics to be allowed to stay at a monastery for a night or two when they are traveling, instead of having to stay at a hotel.

Master Lingyuan was shorter than me, with a big belly and a round face. When he was sitting, he looked like an arhat, one who has achieved enlightenment. He walked very slowly and spoke very gently. Although he seldom smiled, he radiated compassion, so people weren't afraid of him. He usually wore robes with holes and patches. He didn't care if people looked down on him. He didn't have the air of a great monk. He was from Zhejiang, a province on the east coast of China, south of Shanghai, and didn't know much Mandarin. But because I was from Jiangsu, I was able to converse with him.

Despite my uniform, he didn't treat me like a layperson. He heard that because of a lack of space we were going to sleep on the same platform that evening, although laypeople were not supposed to share a sleeping area with monks. "We are going to investigate Chan together this evening," he told me.

When Lingyuan traveled, he didn't care if there was no bed. He just found a place to sit in a cross-legged posture similar to sitting meditation, although he would not sit up straight. He dropped his head forward and slept that way.

Two sutras speak of sleeping yoga. The posture takes practice. Otherwise, when you fall asleep, you will bend your back forward and you won't be able to sleep comfortably. With practice, you can sit up properly and really fall asleep. There are no dreams in this posture, and you can get a good night's rest. When Lingyuan sat this way, he was very stable and looked like a Buddha statue.

We sat together in meditation on the sleeping platform under a huge green mosquito net. Then I reclined and fell into a dreamless sleep that was joyful and relaxed. When I awoke, Lingyuan was still sitting, and I joined him.

Lingyuan rarely spoke except when spoken to. "Can I ask you a question?" I finally blurted out.

"Yes," he replied.

I started with one question, but suddenly there were a hundred, each more perplexing than the last. They poured from my mouth in a torrent of doubt and despair: Would I be able to become a monk again? How would I be able to do that? Which teacher should I go to? What should I do after I became a monk? What kind of monk did I want to become? How would I be able to benefit others, as well as myself, as a monk? With Buddhist teachings as deep and vast as the ocean, where should I start? With innumerable methods of practice, which method should I choose?

On and on I went, hoping this monk, who seemed so free and at ease with himself, would resolve these questions once and for all. But Lingyuan's response was simply to ask me if I had any more questions each time I paused to take a breath.

On and on I went, pouring out my heart, all my pent-up frustration and confusion. Finally, Lingyuan sighed, lifted his hand, and struck the bed hard.

"PUT IT DOWN!" he shouted at me.

It was a shocking, startling command. Suddenly my mind snapped. I poured sweat and felt a great weight lifted from me. In a flash, the cloud and fog dissipated. The hideous miasma of *ku men* that had enveloped me vanished; in its place was a profound sense of well-being. My whole body felt cool and extremely relaxed. Any further questioning seemed unnecessary. There was nothing where my doubts and despair had been, and no problem anywhere in the world. Everything had gone.

I didn't say a word but just sat with Lingyuan. I was extremely happy. The next day the whole world was fresh as if I was seeing it for the first time.

This was my first meeting with a great master. He did not acknowledge me as his student.

"Should I follow you?" I asked before we parted.

"That is your problem," he replied. I received no words of encouragement or direction from him. But after that night, my mind settled.

I still responded to temptation with feelings of desire, hatred, fear, worry, or vanity. But I was able to let go of these mental reactions immediately. Once I let go, I felt very much at ease. For example, later in life, the government wanted to appoint me to a seat in the Congress, an opportunity that many people coveted. I saw it as a temptation and I let it go. Later, when I was in Japan, someone offered me their daughter's hand in marriage and abbotship in a temple during a tense political period when it looked like I might be deported back to Taiwan. I declined. After my encounter with Lingyuan, I knew very clearly what my life was about and how to proceed. I had undergone a tremendous transformation.

Was it karma that brought Master Lingyuan into my life? It's not really karma. Instead, the encounter between me and Lingyuan came from what is called "virtuous roots." Karma refers to the law of cause and effect in Buddhism. So when we say that such and such is happening because of karma, what we mean is that what we are experiencing now is the result of our past actions. If I have been nasty in the past to my neighbor, one cold morning when my car battery is dead and I am late for work she will be unwilling to give me a jump-start. Or if I have been friendly in the past to my neighbor, she will introduce me to a nice contractor to help me build my deck. That is a simple explanation of karma, although when you really start investigating how karma works you realize its dazzling complexity.

Related to karma but somewhat different, virtuous roots refer to the fact that one has engaged in Dharma practice before, thus sowing the seed for an interest in and/or affinity for practice in this life. Very often, we attribute one's ability to meet a good master, or practice well, or understand the Dharma to one's virtuous roots, the fact that one has practiced in previous lives and vowed to practice diligently in future lives.

So-called coincidences are the ripening of the positive affinities formed with others in our past lives. Everyone has done good deeds and formed positive affinities in the past. Some of us don't cultivate them, however, and they don't ripen or emerge. Others cultivate them and allow them to gestate. I cultivated my positive affinities by trying hard to become a monk again. But the opportunity to rejoin the clergy had to do with my virtuous roots and my vows from past lives. Because my vow power was strong, the positive affinities and deeds sowed in the past were able to ripen. Everyone has such affinities and deeds, but if their vow power is weak, they will not ripen easily.

I was on furlough when I encountered Master Lingyuan. I could have followed my friends and had fun. Instead, I went to a monastery to strengthen my practice and read Buddhist scripture. I believe Master Lingyuan was in my past lives, and we had a good affinity. So when I tried to become a monk again in this life, using my vow power, the deepest kind of promise and commitment one can make as a human being, he emerged to help me along the way. Even today, I feel free all the time. There is nothing that binds me, not fame, not money, not power, not women. Although I have myriad responsibilities, I do not feel bound by them.

My experience makes me think of this story: My attendant recently fed me potato leaves. She gave me the soft leaves, and I told her to plant the roots. She planted them casually, and they died after three days. That's because she didn't know how to cultivate them. She dug a hole in rocky, sandy soil. She was perplexed when a potato plant didn't grow. So I taught her how to cultivate the plant. Now it will grow. That was what Master Lingyuan did for me. He taught me how to grow, so I would not die in the harsh soil of army life.

9

Free at Last

When I returned from my furlough at the monastery, I felt renewed and ready to face new opportunities. I was determined to leave the army, in which I had served for almost nine years.

For quite some time I had been submitting essays to *Humanity* magazine, a Buddhist periodical published at the Institute of Buddhist Culture in Beitou, a city near Taibei (Taipei). The publisher, Master Dongchu, liked my writing. I would go to visit him and we developed a friendly connection.

One day out of the blue he said: "You were once a monk. Would you like to be a monk again?"

"Yes," I replied. "I just don't know how."

He didn't say anything.

One Sunday, when I came to visit him, Master Dongchu introduced me to a wealthy woman named Mrs. Zheng.

"This young man is a monk," Master Dongchu said.

Mrs. Zheng looked me over. "He is an officer in uniform. How can he be a monk?"

Master Dongchu told her the story of how I left home at a

young age to become a monk, then had to flee the mainland and enter the army. "So Mrs. Zheng," he said, "do you think there is something that can be done for him?"

"Where is he stationed?" she asked.

"He is the subordinate of your husband, General Zheng Jie-min," Dongchu said.

The general's job at that time was as chief of the Ministry of National Security, a job equivalent to the head of the Central Intelligence Agency in the United States. He reported directly to the president and was responsible for national security.

"Really?" Zheng exclaimed. "He is my husband's subordinate?"

I was in fact an indirect subordinate, officially part of the defense ministry, although I was supervised by the Ministry of National Security, which was interested in the radio transmissions, telephone conversations, telegraphs, and faxes that I intercepted from mainland China. Even after all these years, my job was, in some ways, absurd. I hadn't a clue what anyone was talking about in the coded messages I intercepted. I dutifully submitted them to be decoded by experts at the Ministry of National Security and never once heard anything about them again.

Dongchu told Zheng that I was ill. I have had health problems all my life. Not only did I have both tuberculosis and malaria, which has led to lifelong difficulties with my spleen, when I was ten I fell from a tree and fractured my tailbone. I never told my parents about my tumble for fear that they would scold me for tree climbing, and my spine never properly healed. I also have a neck injury that gives me problems from jumping over a gymnastic horse and falling on my head.

In the military, I suffered from lack of sleep. I frequently worked the night shift and during the day my sleep was fractured by the comings and goings in our communal bedroom. I often gave up on sleeping altogether to read and write essays. Initially I was delighted to have all that time for personal work. But after the first year, lack of sleep caught up with me, dulling my appetite, and I grew thin as a wraith.

Mrs. Zheng told her husband about my situation. She invited me to meet him in their apartment. I went to meet this illustrious and powerful personage without much hope that it would do any good.

General Zheng was an imposing figure, very tall for a Chinese, just under six feet. He was Cantonese, so he spoke Cantonese Mandarin, which was almost impossible for me to understand. His reputation was that he was loyal, incorruptible, and never took bribes. He rarely spoke during our meeting, asking only a few questions. Even his wife was afraid of him.

At the end of our meeting he said: "You are a fine person. How can we let you leave the military, especially when we are in such urgent need of manpower?"

"General Zheng, I am sick," I said.

"What kind of illness? If you truly are sick, you should go to the doctor to certify your condition."

I had to confess that doctors had already refused to certify my condition.

The general was silent at this news and that ended the interview.

Mrs. Zheng, however, was undeterred. She set up an exam at the National Security Ministry, where I told the doctor that I had a chronic condition that was difficult to detect. I was five feet eight inches tall and weighed only ninety-three pounds. I mentioned that I was often dizzy. The doctor agreed that there must be something wrong and checked my blood. He discovered that

I was seriously anemic. I told him about my back problem. He checked my spine and found a problem in my vertebrae. "You must be in a lot of pain when you sit for long periods," he said. He X-rayed my lungs and found dark shadows. He also uncovered problems with my teeth and nose and sent me to a hospital where I got a note to take two three-month medical leaves. I was glad to finally have my illness recognized with X-ray films, test results, and diagnostic records.

I spent my army leave resting in the barracks. After the time was up, my unit wanted me back. I went for more tests, to find my condition had neither improved nor worsened. "That means you are fine and you should go back to work," the doctor said.

I went to Mrs. Zheng and told her what had happened. She called the doctors again and I was granted another six-month medical leave. Anyone who took medical leave for at least a year was eligible to leave the army, so I applied for a dismissal.

My supervisor called me in. "Do you know what we do in this unit?" he asked.

"I know, we do intelligence work," I said.

"That means anyone working in this unit is an intelligence worker when he's alive and he's still an intelligence worker when he's dead."

"I am aware of that rule."

"Because you are engaged in intelligence work, you cannot be a dismissed."

I went again to Mrs. Zheng. "I should qualify to be dismissed and return to monastic life. But my supervisor says no," I said.

"These people are so stubborn," she replied. "I will talk to my husband again. I rarely ask him for help. For you, I will ask him twice. I have never done that. But because I am a Buddhist, I feel that you will contribute more as a monk than an officer. My husband won't think so as he thinks that the military is far more important than Buddhism. Although I am afraid of him, I will approach him again on your behalf."

When people found out that I had met with General Zheng twice, they balked. It was almost impossible for someone of my low rank to meet someone of General Zheng's rank. When I met with Zheng, I was awed by his rank and dignified demeanor. He seemed huge in my eyes, superhuman. Years later, when I returned to Taiwan after becoming a Dharma master and earning my doctorate, the high-level generals I saw no longer looked or felt huge. They looked ordinary. They were older and wore their civilian clothes. They were no different from everyone else, and a number of them actually took refuge with me and became my disciples.

After Mrs. Zheng spoke with him, the general addressed a note to my supervisor on his own official stationery, requesting that my supervisor help me "within the limits of the law." Although I thought that the note was probably useless, I brought it to my supervisor. He scanned it and threw it back at me. "He told me to help you within the limits of the law," he said. "What am I supposed to do?"

A month later, my supervisor's secretary phoned and told me to come in. I thought he was going to jail me. "Here are a few forms," he said. "I don't know if they will help you, but the general said to fill them out anyway. There is no guarantee; we still need to work within the law."

Why bother, I thought? I filled out the forms anyway. And lo and behold, two months later I was dismissed on the grounds of chronic illness. General Zheng died the day before I left the army. I recited sutras for him the day before I was granted my freedom and given back my life.

The entire petitioning process for dismissal spanned eighteen months, an interminable time when you're young and waiting for something you want with all your heart. Looking back, I realize that if I didn't have a very strong will to return to monastic life, I probably wouldn't have succeeded. Getting out of my particular branch of the military was nearly impossible.

On January 1, 1960, I officially left the military. I was thirty years old.

10

"The filial son is produced under the cane"

I first met Master Dongchu long before I began writing essays for his magazine, *Humanity*, while I was still in the army. He was quite famous in mainland China as the abbot of Jiao-shan's Dinghui Monastery (Monastery of Samadhi and Wisdom) in Zhenjiang, the capital of Jiangsu Province. Jiaoshan's Dinghui, a very famous Chan monastery in China, was first built around 194–195 C.E. and changed its name several times, finally becoming Dinghui Monastery during the Qing dynasty (1644–1911 C.E.). It is on an island in the Yangzi River, on a hill several hundred meters high that is called the Floating Jade Mountain.

Dongchu came to a conference at the Buddhist institute in Shanghai while I was studying there. Some of his former students called him "Big Gun" because he bellowed, especially when he scolded people, which he often did. He was a progressive thinker and would attack people who had stale ideas. Students were so afraid of him that they would transfer out of his institute to study in Shanghai.

My first impression of Dongchu was striking. He was a hulking man with a square, dignified face who carried himself like a patriarch although he was only in his forties. He walked like a general, as if he created wind in his wake, yet he was extremely stable. None of us kids dared to speak to him.

Dongchu had arrived in Taiwan before I had, but I did not think of seeking him out because there were so many other Dharma masters from the mainland whom I wanted to see. Then Xingru, a classmate from Shanghai who worked as the editor for Dongchu's *Humanity* magazine, asked me to submit material to the publication. My reputation as a writer was growing, and I had published short novels, poems, and essays under the pen name Xing Shi Jiang Jun ("World-Awakening General"). The money I made from writing for *Humanity* was several times my army salary. I soon became a regular contributor, but didn't meet Dongchu until the editor introduced us on Buddha's Birthday. At this event, which was organized by the Chinese Buddhist Federation, we set a little statue of the infant Buddha in a basin of water and each devotee bowed and poured water over the Buddha's head. This ceremony reminded us that bodhi mind is born in us every moment, giving us a chance to renew bodhi mind and cultivate the path of Buddhahood.

"Do you want to meet with Master Dongchu?" the editor asked me. "He is here, and I can take you to see him."

"He hasn't asked to see me," I said.

"Yes, he did. He said that he would like to meet you when he has a chance."

The editor introduced me. "This is the World-Awakening General," he said to Master Dongchu.

"I have seen you, but you don't know me," I offered.

Master Dongchu did not seem particularly excited to meet me, but he did say, "Come visit when you have time."

The following week, I paid him a visit at the Institute of Buddhist Culture, which he had founded. Books filled the shelves along all the walls, and I hoped I would get the chance to read them one by one. It was rare at that time to find so many Buddhist books, especially the Tripitaka, the three canons consisting of the sutras (the Buddha's sermons), the vinaya (rules of discipline), and sastras (treatises on the Buddha's teachings). Also present on the shelves was the *Book of Twenty-five Histories of China.* There were also other books on religion, philosophy, calligraphy, and painting.

Master Dongchu was gracious, although somewhat aloof. He fed me well, received me in a friendly manner, and asked about army life. When I left, he gave me a red envelope with money in it. I was really grateful; he had seemed cold, but he had given me so much money!

"When you have leave, you can come here," he said. "We don't have great food or fun things to do, but we have books here and you are always welcome."

So I began to visit Dongchu often and worked on essays for his magazine. We didn't talk about my future, but I had a feeling that he was watching me.

I told Dongchu that when I left the army I would like to return to monastic life.

"That's good," he said.

"But where should I go?" I asked.

"I don't know," he said. "It's your choice."

That gave me the impression that he didn't want me as a disciple. So I visited the great masters one by one and they were all willing to accept me. Only one, Master Nanting, said no. He was a Dharma brother to Master Dongchu since they had shared the same master. "I have a grand disciple now and he is older than you," he said. "This temple is small and if I accept you as my disciple, how should he treat you since he is already a Dharma teacher? You would be his senior."

"Where should I go to become a monk again?" I asked.

"You are so silly! Master Dongchu has helped you. Be grateful and go to him to become his disciple immediately!"

"He didn't say that he wanted me."

"You have to beg him to take you. Kneel down and ask him to accept you!"

I felt like a moron as I went back to see Dongchu in Beitou, as though I was still the sickly child from a little village way out in the middle of nowhere who collected dung in the fields and fell out of trees and couldn't speak until he was five.

When I arrived at Dongchu's place, I didn't know how to begin. I had the same feeling of teetering on the brink as I had had when I left home to go to Wolf Mountain and leaned forward into the wind on the prow of the paddleboat on the way to Shanghai.

"Master Dongchu," I began self-consciously, with not just a little trepidation. "I couldn't find any master to take me in. Many people are willing to accept me, but I don't really want to go with any of them. And the place I really want to go wouldn't accept me." I recounted my meeting with Master Nanting.

Dongchu looked at me with his dignified demeanor and wide impassive face, saying nothing, waiting. It was no good. I knew I had to throw myself on his mercy. I summoned up all the times that he had shown an interest in me, and his generosity toward me when he had given me money. I was teetering on the brink and then I jumped, crumpling to my knees, prostrating myself before him, begging him to take me in as a monk. It was an unseemly display of emotion, but I felt as if my life was on the line, and all those long years I had spent in the army, yearning to be back in monastic life, were pushing my forehead toward the floor and forcing out the abject, begging words of pleading and longing and need from my mouth.

Dongchu reprimanded me. "Get up, get up!" he said, but didn't say whether he would take me in so I remained on my knees. "I am grateful for the master's help," I said. "Since I've spent so much time here, I am really quite close to the old master."

"Where will you go after you become a monk?" Dongchu finally asked. "This place is so small."

"I have nowhere to go after becoming a monk," I said.

"If you don't mind that this place is so small, you can try it out here," he said. But I noticed that he still had not definitively said whether I could become a monk under him, committing to the ancient relationship of master and disciple.

"I really want to become a monk as soon as possible," I said, pressing him. I really felt at that moment as if I had nowhere else to go and by begging him on my knees I had taken an irrevocable, fateful step.

He nodded. "Okay. I will find a good time to have your head shaved."

I rose to my feet with a feeling of gratitude and elation and bowed to him in thanks.

Dongchu was hosting a seven-day Buddha-name recitation retreat. He invited several monks from out of town to help with the Dharma instruments. On the second to last day of the ceremony, he said to me, "I will shave your head tomorrow."

"Tomorrow?" I replied. "I don't even have monk's robes."

"What monk's robes? When we became monks, we just picked up rags from other people."

He asked the other monks if they had any old monk's robes for me. The monks knew me by my pen name, the World-

Awakening General. Some of them were classmates from China. "We will exhaust our means to find him clothes," they said.

They went home that night and returned the next morning with all sorts of clothing, including robes and undergarments. Most were too big or too long.

"These clothes don't fit," I said to my master.

"Monastics in the past all wore other people's old clothes," he said. "If they could alter them, they altered them. If that was not possible, they just wore what they could get. In Shakyamuni Buddha's time, they went to the cemetery to pick up the cloth used for wrapping corpses and washed them and wore them. These clothes that you have been given are just fine."

I understood and took the clothes. Some were too short and only reached my belly button or shins. But I wore them.

The devotees for the name recitation ceremony had gone, and only two monks remained.

"Now I will shave your head," said Master Dongchu.

"There should be some witnesses," I objected. "We should allow some of the laypeople to stay to witness the head shaving ceremony."

"I knew all along that you are no good," Master Dongchu said harshly, glaring at me. "You are so vain. It is your second time to become a monk and you are thirty years old! When I was thirty, I was already an abbot."

There wasn't much I could say to that! On January 6, 1960, Dongchu shaved my head and gave me the name Huikong Shengyan. "Shengyan" is the proper pinyin spelling, but I use "Sheng Yen" now because that is how I am known. A very small group attended the shaving ceremony. Only one master attended as a guest—Master Lianhang.

So my training began. Prior to the ceremony, Dongchu had never scolded me. It was apt that he scolded me as he accepted me back into the monastic fold, for there were to be many more scoldings to come.

I moved into the smallest of the institute's three rooms. After several days, as I was settling in, Dongchu told me to move into the large room. "You are a writer and like to read," he said. "You should have more space to read and write."

I happily moved all my possessions into the big room. The next day he told me: "Your karmic obstruction is heavy. I'm afraid that you may not have enough virtuous karma to stay in the big room. I think it's better you move back to the small room."

I was peeved—I had just moved in. But because it was his request, I complied. A few days later, he came to me and said, "You know what? You should move to the big room. You are right, you really need it for your books and to have enough space to write."

"Master, don't worry," I said. "I can stay in the small room. There is no need to move."

"It's my order. You should move to the big room." He looked at me with his big square face and grave demeanor, turned on his heels, and walked away with his general's walk, leaving wind in his wake.

I moved. I wasn't even there for even half a day when Dongchu appeared at my door. "You are right," he said. "It's better for you to live in the small room. You don't need to move your stuff in there. Just move there to sleep."

Another couple of days passed, and he told me to move all my things to the small room. There was a lot to move, and it took a long time. A few days later, we received a guest. Late that night, Dongchu knocked on my door. "It's better for our guest to sleep in the small room. Why don't you move to the big room for tonight?" he said.

Later he told me it would be better to keep the small room

open for guests, so I should move to the big room. At this point, I lost my temper. "Why do you keep asking me to move from one room to the other?" I whined. "I have already moved five times! I'm not going to move anymore!"

"This is my order!" he bellowed, a mountain of a man who had been one of the most famous abbots on the mainland. "I asked you to move, so you must move!"

I skulked off and started the onerous process of transferring my possessions yet again. I had no choice: This is the way it is in the master-disciple relationship—the disciple must do whatever the master asks.

Dongchu kept asking me to move, and eventually I got it through my thick head that this was part of my training, so I stopped protesting and just moved. Once I just acted, without hesitation, protest, or resentment, Dongchu let me stay put.

I soon fell into the daily rhythms of the institute. There were meditation sessions each morning and evening. After morning service and before dinner, we worked in the garden, Dongchu included. Two nuns, Dingxin Shi and Jianxin Shi, also lived at the institute. We used roots, peels, and old leaves as our fertilizer, along with a mixture of urine and feces taken from the pit underneath our brick outhouse. Now we would consider this process unhygienic, but our vegetables were beautiful and the garden produced for us. Dongchu's garden was in my mind many years later when I established the Nung Chan (Farm and Chan) Monastery in Taibei with its extensive vegetable garden and orchard.

Our material life was very simple. The best food we ate was bean curd. We had fermented bean curd at breakfast, with rice porridge. Each week, we bought two blocks of tofu, which we thinly sliced. Dongchu allowed each of us one cubic inch of the bean curd, the same amount he limited to himself. But he supplemented his with special food offered by his followers. He had salted, roasted peanuts, ten at each meal. When I saw him eat a mouthful of rice after each peanut, I envied his luxury.

When my old classmate stopped editing *Humanity* magazine, I took over, writing editorials and essays, handling letters from readers, receiving and sending back manuscripts, and doing copyediting, design, and layout. I learned from scratch. I didn't know anything about using different font styles and sizes. The printing press workers weren't much help. They did no copyediting. Some were illiterate, and each time they set up a page, I had to copyedit it three times. Even so there were errors.

But the more difficult issue with the magazine was politics. We were not allowed to print any criticism of the government or its policies. We had to be very careful about using the first character of the term "communist," although sometimes the workers put it in by mistake. We had to be exceedingly careful with essays that touched on political issues.

Once the magazine was printed, I was responsible for mailing it to subscribers. Although we required subscriptions, we often sent the magazine out for free to Buddhist groups. My salary was $200 Taiwanese, about five U.S. dollars, which covered transportation, travel, meals, postage, and other expenses.

"Don't edit the magazine for your master anymore," an acquaintance advised. "The amount of money he pays you for editing it for a month is one day's pay for a carpenter or mason." People would always tell me to make money by reciting sutras for the dead. You could bring in $200 a day. However, I knew from past experience that it was too easy to fall into bad habits when you don't have time to practice and have money to burn. My efforts were met with derision. "You are educated and have no money," people said. "You edit a magazine and only make $200 a month, and it's not even for you."

I told my master about these jeers. "If monastics think about money, they should not be monastics," he said. "Monastics are here to contribute." I understood.

Dongchu encouraged me to read sutras, write essays, and do outreach in the community. "You should teach whatever Dharma you know," he said. "If you just stay in the monastery, you are being passive."

The monastery had very few visitors, and there were very few people teaching the Dharma in Taiwan at the time. Dongchu wanted me to carry sacred texts and teach the contents to people waiting at bus stops. He wanted me to share *Humanity* magazine with strangers on the street and give public lectures. Basically, he wanted me to copy the approach of Christian evangelicals, who were indeed very successful. They would even come to the monastery to spread Christian teachings!

Dongchu continued to test me in ways that took me some time to understand. When I was sent to buy rice and oil, he would give me just enough money for the purchase without enough to cover the cost of transportation. A bag of rice was too heavy for me to carry, and I had to beg truck drivers to give me a lift. When my master found out about this, he said: "That's good. You are giving the people who help you opportunities to create merit."

What kind of merit are they creating, I thought? They are just helping me this time. After this time, they won't come back. But I had learned not to cross Dongchu and didn't say anything.

When I was sent to a distant place, such as central Taiwan,

for one thing or another, Dongchu would only give me half the car fare.

"It's not enough," I told him.

"You are so dumb!" he scolded. "With what you have, you can get a ticket for half the way. Once on board the bus or train, you can pretend to be asleep and make it the whole way."

Dongchu wanted to save money, but he also wanted to see how I would handle the situation. Traveling beyond the distance allowed by my ticket, I was once chased off a bus—a humiliating experience. From that point on, I begged other passengers to help pay for the full price of my tickets, which didn't cost all that much. Dongchu approved. "You are getting these people to practice Dharma," he said.

Dongchu didn't have much money—just a pittance from a few followers and whatever he could earn by printing and selling copies of sutras. I came to realize that he sent me out without enough money as his way of training, which can be likened to keeping bees instead of birds. Pet birds must be fed, so they forget how to be independent. Bees are not fed, but the beehive is kept in a place with flowers nearby so that the bees will go out and make honey. This way, the bees not only get their own food, but they can also produce honey to be sold.

One day my master ordered me to do prostrations to the Buddha. After a couple of days of prostrations, he said to me, "This is a Buddhist institute. You are not doing anything to contribute. You should write some essays."

Everything he asked me to write involved scolding people. "If I am scolding people all the time, everyone is going to hate me," I said.

"You can use your pen name. Since you are a new monk, you should speak up to uphold justice."

I wrote scolding essays. After he read them, Dongchu said, "You are terrible! You are scolding people too much." He didn't publish any of them.

"You have committed much speech karma in scolding so many people," he said. "You should go do prostrations to repent."

I went back to doing prostrations. One day he bellowed at me: "What are you doing wasting time prostrating to a wooden statue! It's useless. You should go read some real sutras."

He told me to read the big sutras, not the small ones. The *Avatamsaka (Huayan) Sutra* has eighty chapters, the *Nirvana Sutra* forty, and *Mahaprajnaparamita Sutra* six hundred! I started in on the *Mahaprajnaparamita*.

After a few days, Dongchu asked how many chapters I'd read. I told him thirty; I was a very slow reader.

"You are so slow!" he bellowed. "Too much karmic obstruction. There is no use reading when you read like a worm crawls. Go do prostrations to the Buddha to give rise to some wisdom."

So I did prostrations; after a few days, Dongchu berated me again. "Sheng Yen! Look at yourself. What you are doing is of absolutely no use. You should do something concrete to make yourself useful. You and your bowing is like a dog eating shit."

"What should I do?" I asked.

He pointed to a pile of bricks. The individual bricks had been mortared together. "Each piece of brick that made up that wall was a contribution from our followers. It is such a waste for them to sit there idle. You should go and rearrange the bricks."

I took the bricks apart carefully and put them in a neat pile, so they would be ready for whatever use Dongchu had in mind. I worked in this way for several days and felt quite good about my progress. But when Dongchu saw what I had done, he scolded me. "I told you to arrange the bricks, but you are so useless! The bricks were already in good shape, but you've broken them up in fragments! You need to assemble them again."

I looked at the pile of broken bricks and thought: this is so awful, so pointless, so tedious. There was no way I could piece the bricks back together. "I don't know how to go about this," I protested. "It's impossible to put the pieces back together."

"You are useless!" responded Dongchu in a harsh tone, looking at me with his stern unyielding face, arms crossed over his big body. "Have you heard about looking for a needle in a haystack? *That's* impossible. Why is it impossible to put the bricks back together so that we can make good use of them?"

From then on, Dongchu didn't ask me to do prostrations, or write essays, or read sutras. I had to put the brick pieces back together. I felt it was such a waste of time. I mustered my courage. "Is it really worth the time to put these bricks back together?" I finally asked Dongchu.

"What is your time worth?" he replied. "You live here for free and eat for free. What is the problem? Go and reassemble the bricks. Don't be wasteful."

Those were the orders of my master, so I continued on with the bricks. At first, I was at a total loss, but then, miraculously, it became easier. I could see how the bricks fit together. I could piece together three bricks a day; it took me fifteen days to do them all. I had no idea what he was going to do with the bricks when I was finished. I just did it.

When I was done, Master told me, "Now stack up the bricks."

"How?" I asked. "These bricks have been broken. They won't hold up." But he insisted. I was puzzled, and I went outside to take a break. As I walked around, an idea came to me. I saw the large leaves of the wild taro. I put several pieces of bricks on a leaf, then put another taro leaf with bricks on top of it. Now I could pile the bricks on top of each other without having them crumble. It took me several months to get it done, and each day I wanted to run away, so tedious and ridiculous was the work.

When the bricks were finished, Dongchu treated me to one of his rare moments of mirth. "You have been tricked!" He laughed. "Ho, ho, ho." His big belly shook. He was really enjoying himself. "These bricks are useless!" he said. "You must be mad at me over this."

"I was a bit mad," I admitted, sulking.

"But you are not so bad," he said. "You are actually quite patient."

Perhaps because I had demonstrated patience, Dongchu let me live in peace for a few months. But then one day he pointed at a spot in the kitchen where the ceramic tiles had fallen off. "Sheng Yen, you have to fix this," he commanded. "Go to the construction material company and buy exactly the same tiles and replace the ones that are missing."

Well and good. This didn't seem to be such a difficult task. I was always being sent on these types of minor errands. Little did I know the ordeal in store for me.

I went into town and bought what I thought were the same tiles. When I returned, my master said, "Come and look. These are not quite the same. You must return them and buy identical ones."

I looked closely at the tiles. Indeed, although the new ones I had bought were very close in appearance to the old tiles, they were not identical. However, you only noticed this upon extremely close inspection. What possible difference could it make? I was about to protest, but one look at Dongchu's face told me to shut my trap. Off I went to the tile shop again. They were not pleased to see me. I had bought only three tiles and now I was returning them! They refused to help me find the right tiles. This, I knew, was not a good result, but what could I do? I went back to Dongchu. "Master," I said, "I couldn't find the same tiles."

"Why not?" he asked.

"The people in the tile shop refused to look for just three tiles."

"And this means you are giving up? You are an imbecile. Go find out which kiln made the tiles."

I went to construction material companies all over town, asking the absurd question about which kiln had made these three obscure and completely unremarkable tiles. No one was the least bit interested. Predictably, I got nowhere and began to feel frustrated and full of resentment and self-pity. Finally, by a stroke of luck, I ran into a kiln worker, and he told me where the kiln was for which he worked, although he was not sure if it was the one that had fired my tiles.

I went to the kiln. Mounted on the wall were rows of tiles, but I couldn't find an exact match. I asked the clerk at the kiln if he could make the tiles for me. He asked me how many I needed and I told him three.

"We are wholesale," he said. "I can't sell you only three pieces."

"Please help me," I begged. "Dongchu insisted that I get three pieces of the same tiles as those we have on the wall of our kitchen."

"Every batch of tiles is slightly different in color," he explained. "There is no way you can get three tiles of identical color." The clerk told me about another kiln, far away.

"Could I find the same tiles there?" I asked.

"How would I know?"

I felt utterly hopeless. I went back to my master, telling him that the task was impossible.

"Each batch of tiles is slightly different in color," I explained, without hope that this would be the end of it.

"Yesterday," he said, "I found out where the tiles came from."

"How do I get there?"

"You are really a moron! You can ask for directions on the way to the shop."

The place was very remote and quite far away. It took me most of one day, begging my bus fare and wandering around on foot to finally find it. I asked about the tiles. "We make lots of tiles," the man in charge said. "How are we supposed to know whether we made these tiles? How many do you want?"

"Three pieces," I said.

They looked at me as if I had lost my mind. "You came all the way here for three pieces of tile? We're too busy to sell you three pieces. You should go to a construction material company."

I left without any tiles. They must think I'm crazy, I thought on my way home, when it was really my master who was crazy, making such unreasonable requests.

"They wouldn't sell me three pieces," I told Dongchu.

"You are a dolt! All you have to do is ask which construction material company buys their products and get the tiles from that company. You should have asked while you were there and gone and done it. Wouldn't that have been easy? And then we wouldn't be having this conversation."

"It's just a few pieces of tile," I groaned, too tired and frustrated to keep my feelings bottled up any longer. I felt like a thirty-year-old child. I was an officer in the army, for goodness' sake, a published author, and here I was scouring Taiwan for tiles. "Why can't we just buy three pieces that are close in color? It's just kitchen tile."

"Excuse me," he said. "If I put these two bandages on your face and leave them there forever, is that okay?"

I glared at him and said nothing. Dongchu ordered me to go out to look for the tiles. I wandered around, not going anywhere in particular, brooding on Dongchu's unreasonable requests. I made up my mind to leave the monastery.

When I returned, I went straight to my room; I was frustrated to the point of being numb. Dongchu popped his head in. "Where have you been all day?" he asked. I refused to talk to him.

He left my room, and came back with three tiles. "We are so lucky!" he exclaimed. "I found three tiles left over from the last kitchen renovation. They were stuck in a crack in the wall." He looked at me and laughed. "Ho, ho, ho." It was a ghastly sound. "You are tricked again!" he said. "You are a monk. How can you get mad? I got you again. That's so funny. Ho, ho, ho." And he left the room.

I should have been furious, but, oddly, my frustration dissolved. I sat in my room after he had left, empty and at peace. I realized that I had no desire to leave Dongchu. I realized that the search for the tiles had been part of the training.

Dongchu read me like a book. He responded to my internal change and the next day was really nice to me. Some visitors brought us fabric from the Philippines.

"Sheng Yen," he said. "You have been a monk for a while, and I haven't given you much. Here is a gift of fabric to make you a robe." He had one of the visitors take my measurements. I felt the warmth of his love deeply. How could I have thought of leaving? Why had I become so frustrated and full of resentment? I still have this piece of clothing after forty-five years.

When I started training with my master, I thought he had a dual personality. But then I realized he was quite consistent in his approach to his students. He treated his students at the Buddhist Institute in Jaoshan the same way he treated me. That's why they were so afraid of him. He believed that a monastic needed to be able to handle pressure. That was the way that he had been trained by his own master. Chinese people believe that "the filial son is produced under the cane," and "masters and patriarchs are produced under the incense board." The training squeezes your ego and pride so that they have nowhere to go, and then they are gone.

In ancient times, all Chan masters trained their promising students this way. They were easier on the students who didn't have as much potential. Like Jesus said, the sheep that are straying need to be held and taken care of. Likewise, in Japan, employees get the "training of the devil" in order to be shaped into good employees.

Although Dongchu tortured me, he wasn't a devil all day long. He liked to joke around, commanding me to sit in a certain way in his presence, with my palms together and back straight, or stand with my palms joined and my head bowed. I could never quite tell if his commands were, at root, a farce. I dared not cross him, yet he constantly reminded me not to become fearful around him. Now I teach my disciples the same thing. I don't want them to indulge themselves when I'm not around, then join their palms together in my presence, just out of fear.

Through Dongchu's training, I learned much about myself. I had a tendency to resist what I perceived to be unfair and become vexed over things that I considered unreasonable. I was able to eliminate such habits. After training with Dongchu, I viewed life from a less self-centered perspective. I tried to understand why things happened in a certain way, but I wasn't bothered by it so much. I also didn't feel ashamed as much. At first it was a really shameful and embarrassing thing to be chased off a bus. But after the training, I considered such situations an opportunity to practice.

After two years with Dongchu, I decided to go into solitary retreat in the mountains. I told myself that would help me do something for Buddhism. I vowed not to be selfish, practicing merely for my own liberation. I would instead follow the Mahayana teaching to "deliver others before one is delivered. This is the initial arising of bodhi mind of a bodhisattva." I told my master I would practice hard so as not to fail the Dharma.

"The important thing is not to fail yourself!" he said.

I didn't know what he meant. I pondered these words for a long time before I realized that Dongchu saw that I was still selfish, even though I thought my vows were for others. He saw that my departure from household life and my vow to deliver sentient beings might have been nothing more than empty words. He was pushing me to take responsibility for myself, to understand the responsibilities of a monastic. If I didn't fulfill my responsibilities and do what I was supposed to do, I would be failing myself. That was what he meant.

He wanted me to live a true monastic life, uphold the precepts, cultivate samadhi, give rise to wisdom, maintain a charitable mind, and endure difficulties. He did not want me to make empty vows, but rather to understand my original vows—why I had originally chosen to become a monk.

In Chinese Chan tradition, there is a saying: "When the heels do not touch the ground while traveling the world in the four directions, this is dangerous."

My master's advice was right. So when I train my disciples, I don't ask them to become a great Chan master, a famous Dharma master, or an accomplished monastic. I want them to work on three things. The first is developing a proper monastic attitude. The second is carrying oneself with proper monastic de-meanor; monastics have very different posture, facial expressions, and gestures from laypeople. The third is speaking properly; monastics don't use foul language, slang, or street talk. We don't speak frivolously, chatting away about meaningless things.

Proper monastic behavior—this is what my master meant by not failing oneself. It can take ten years just to develop the proper attitude. The old monks from the previous generation like to say that during the first ten years of monastic life, you don't even know in your dreams if you are a layman or a monastic. In dreams, you are still allowed to do things that laypeople do. After ten years, you won't forget that you're a monastic, not even in your dreams.

I have a female disciple who wanted to become a monastic. She lived at the Chan Meditation Center in New York for more than a year when it was first established. One day she came in to see me and told me that she couldn't continue on the monastic path.

"Why not?" I asked.

"It's embarrassing. I don't think I should say," she said.

"Why not? What kind of bad things are you doing?"

"In my dreams, I was with my boyfriend and we indulged ourselves and had sex. How can I become a monastic?"

"As long as you are not with a man having sex in the day-time, that is fine, because that's when you have control over yourself," I said. "You can't control yourself in your dreams because you haven't been in training long enough."

I asked her if she still wanted to become a monastic. "I will try," she replied.

A few days later, she told me she was having the same dream again.

"It will be a while before you can eliminate such mental habits and attitudes," I said. "They may persist even after you become a monastic."

This is the attitude I teach. It isn't easy. Only through practice will you firmly cultivate in your mind that you are a monastic. Otherwise, you will still be a layperson in your dreams, even after a hundred years of living in a monastery and studying the Dharma.

11

Wild Potato Leaves

The Zhaoyuan Monastery, in which I went on solitary retreat, was at the very southern tip of Taiwan, planted at the foot of the pyramid-shaped Sharp Mountain and surrounded by wild growth, vines and twisting trees, dense forest, jungle, really, that characterizes the southern part of the island with its hot, humid climate that makes you feel as though you were in the Philippines or the South Seas.

Dongchu had not expected me to leave so soon. I had only been with him for about two years. There was no one left at Dongchu's place to do my chores or run *Humanity* magazine, which had to stop operation. But I had a deep desire to devour Buddhist literature, to repent and read and immerse myself without any distractions. I felt that to have a proper understanding of Buddhist texts was essential for practice. The common wisdom was that people who practiced meditation didn't need to know Buddhist theory. This was not at all my sense. I felt that practitioners needed to be grounded in theory, and I wanted to spend my time on retreat organizing and making accessible to people the vast jumble of Buddhist texts and doctrine.

I came to solitary retreat in the following way. Early in 1961 I had learned that Master Daoyuan would host a full precept ceremony later that year. I asked Dongchu's permission to participate, for, although Dongchu had shaved my head, I had not been formally ordained nor received the full monastic precepts. At the same time, I told Dongchu that I planned to enter solitary retreat after the ceremony. He objected. I prostrated to Guanyin each day to repent for my karmic obstructions so that I could participate in the ordination ceremony and enter retreat.

Dongchu was not the only one who did not support my decision to enter solitary retreat. Master Nanting, who had been very generous to me while I was in the army, also felt that I should not leave Dongchu. Furthermore, he thought that it would be impossible for me to get the necessary financial support for a retreat. At the time, Master Zhiguang offered to sponsor me at the rate of one thousand New Taiwanese dollars per year. I planned to finance my retreat using the money I had received from the army, a bit over ten thousand New Taiwanese dollars, which I thought would be enough for three or four years. Thus, I did not accept Master Zhiguang's offer.

Over the following months, I struggled with whether or not I should leave the institute. I felt an obligation to Dongchu. But I also felt that to leave home is to leave behind worldly attachments, the emotional ties that bind us. I was grateful to Dongchu for helping me become a monk again. His help had been like a bridge that had allowed me to cross a river. But if I were to cling to the bridge because of emotion, then I would have wasted time that should have been used to pursue my goal.

Although I had made up my mind, I still suffered. I was Dongchu's only disciple. I felt like an ingrate, but I had to go.

On November 11, 1961, I bid farewell to Dongchu. Dongchu was surprisingly happy and tried to give me some money. I felt ashamed to take it. Dongchu walked me to the door, not saying a word. I looked back several times, a dog with his tail between his legs. Dongchu was standing silently by the door, watching me go.

It turned out the money from the army that I had counted on for my retreat had been borrowed by a classmate with whom I had studied in Shanghai. He disappeared. So I pieced together support for my retreat from a number of places and went to the far reaches of southern Taiwan to read and write and practice, and make up for all the years that I had lost.

A stream came winding down off the steep slope of Sharp Mountain (Jian Shan, also known as Daxiong Shan) between Zhaoyuan Monastery and the populated plains that stretched toward the Taiwan Strait. The stream was a barrier, effectively sealing off the monastery from the outside world during the rainy season. When the monsoons came, the stream filled with water funneling off the mountain, running waist-deep, high and rushing. The old monks and nuns wouldn't cross the stream, fearing that they would be swept away. Only the younger monastics would venture across it, returning with supplies and news of the outside world.

This stream protected the monastery from being disturbed by outsiders and made it a great place to practice. There were no tourists, no worshippers, no one coming to burn incense. It was a remote, secluded, private place.

The monastery had three rows of houses built along a slope.

When I first arrived, I didn't have my own living space for the solitary retreat. I lived in the attic of the monastery's guesthouse.

Lichee trees and bamboo filled the hillside behind the guesthouse. The monastics harvested lichees and sold them to buy groceries and supplies. They also cultivated a kind of thorny bamboo, harvesting the delicious shoots when they were three to four inches thick, salting and drying them for sale. In the monastery's garden they grew radishes, carrots, bok choy, spinach, cabbage, tang-hao (a leafy green), wild potato (yam) leaves, and betelnut, a plant often chewed by old people. Life was very simple, and the monastics lived on the fruit, bamboo, and vegetables they grew.

When the trees around the monastery were blooming, the air was filled with fragrance. We had so many jade orchids, an extremely fragrant flower, that we sold them in town. We also ate the flowers by battering and deep-frying them. I ate so much jade orchid that my body emitted the sweet odor of the flower!

There was also a tropical plant related to the cactus that produced flowers on its stem that we put in soup, which tasted like slimy okra. There was a delicious bean that grew wild on ten-foot-tall trees, which I would pick when I went into the mountains.

The first half-year was the initial stage of my retreat, during which I adapted to life in the mountains. Each day, I woke at sunrise. In the monastery, we didn't have clocks or watches—we followed the sun. The roosters crowing in the village down the slope and across the stream woke me up. They crowed three times: first when the sun rose, second, at around 9:00 A.M., when the sun was shining in the east, and, third, in the afternoon, around 4:00 P.M., when the sun was heading west.

The monks hit the drum when it was time to wake up. Be

fore lunch, they hit the gong and the wooden fish. Before bed-time, they hit the gong and the drum. So I didn't need a watch or clock. All I needed to do was listen for these sounds and I knew what time it was and what I should be doing.

Half a year after I arrived, my solitary retreat hut was built next to the monastery. I got up when I heard the roosters each morning, washed, drank a glass of water, prostrated to the Bud-dha for about ten minutes, and sat in meditation for an hour. Then I recited the sutras for morning service, which took about an hour, and did repentance prostrations for two-and-a-half hours. After lunch and a short rest, I did another two-and-a-half-hour session of repentance prostrations. Evening service fol-lowed, and dinner. After dinner, I took a shower and meditated. The gong and drum sounded, and I knew that it was time to rest.

The monastery had been built in 1911 of mountain clay and grass that the monks gathered and made into bricks with a wooden mold. The bricks were not baked in a kiln. The walls were two bricks thick. On the outside wall, the bricks were stacked horizontally and on the inside vertically, a wall design that insulates well so that the rooms were cool in the summer and warm in winter. The main pillars of the building were made of tree trunks and the smaller pillars from bamboo stems, which were harvested from the mountain. This was the way they built two-story structures, with relatively low ceilings.

The main beam of the roof was a tree trunk. The side beams were side-by-side lengths of bamboo with gaps between them. On top of the bamboo were two layers of tiles, one layer facing down and the other facing up. This kept the rain out.

Although the design of the buildings was practical and comfortable in many ways, it made for countless cracks, crevices, nooks, and crannies, which were inhabited by a host of sentient beings. There were no screens on the wooden windows, and when they were open, which was most of the time, an astound ing variety of insects came in. Sharp Mountain was as rich in insect life as it was in flora. Bats flitted overhead and small lizards darted across the walls and ceiling, catching mosquitoes and other flying bugs.

Once, a snake, thicker than my arm, appeared on the roof's main beam in my room. Its head hung down, and it stayed that way for half a day without moving. At first it flicked its tongue in and out, and later even that stopped. It looked like it was suffering. We fetched a snake catcher from the village. He was delighted when he saw the snake's size, thinking that it would make a nice dinner.

"Please don't kill this snake," I pleaded. "It has been suffering in my room."

The people in the monastery collected money to give to the snake catcher so that he would let the snake live.

There were also mice. There was nothing in my space for mice to eat, but they visited me anyway, eyeing me while they scampered along the roof beams. When I did repentance prostrations, I prayed for them, since they were also sentient beings. I prayed that they would be reborn as human beings so that they, too, could practice.

Repentance prostrations were a major part of my practice. Prostrations are helpful if you have serious karmic impediments or an unstable mind. I believed that I had very heavy past karmic obstructions because I had been in the army for ten years. So I prostrated to Guanyin and repented. It wasn't that I did bad things while I was in the army, but the people I encountered and what I heard and did were not in accordance with monastic life.

Although I have been at great pains to tell you how careful I was to pick the meat out of dishes, in truth there were times in the army that we were given meat with no vegetables. I ate meat sometimes because I couldn't go without food, but I felt terrible because I believed that I had done something unwholesome.

In the army, I was also exposed to the lives of laypeople. I heard what they said and saw what they did. After hearing and seeing so much, although I didn't behave like them, their behaviors seemed normal to me. My fellow soldiers were always chattering about women, alcohol, and gambling. They changed girlfriends frequently and started fistfights at the drop of a hat. After a few years in the army, when I dreamed at night, I dreamed as a soldier not as a monk. That was the natural outgrowth of the energy of habit and proximity.

Now, I mainly worked with the Dabei chan, or "Repentance of the Great Compassionate," when I prostrated. A Tiantai master of the Song dynasty invented it. With each prostration, I recited the name of a different Buddha or bodhisattva, but Avalokiteshvara was the central figure. At first I did about a dozen prostrations, each one with a Buddha or Bodhisattva's name. Then, while kneeling, I recited a text and prostrated, praising the merits of Bodhisattva Avalokiteshvara. I chanted the Great Compassionate Dharani (eighty-two lines) twenty-one times with my hands joined while slowly walking in a circle around the periphery of the room. After I had chanted the Dharani, I kneeled and praised the power and function of the mantra. I recited Buddha, Dharma, Sangha of the ten directions, the names of Shakyamuni Buddha and Amitabha Buddha, the bodhisattvas—Avalokitesh-

vara, Mahasthama (Dashizhi), and Dharani (King Tuoluoni)—
each three times. Then I recited taking refuge in the Buddha,
Dharma, and Sangha. The recitation lasted one-and-a-half hours.
Doing it, I visualized each item slowly. For example, when I was
praising the merits of Bodhisattva Avalokiteshvara, I visualized
those merits. Praising the power of the mantra, I visualized that
power.

Because I wanted a firm understanding of the basics of Buddhism, I read the Nikayas, the sutras of early Buddhism, as well
as the Agamas, the sutras of later Mahayana Buddhism, and also
the Vinayas, the code of conduct spoken by Shakyamuni Buddha
to his disciples. I read the Vinayas first. The Vinayas consist of
450 books, each having 10,000 words, for a total of 4.5 million
words. Then I read the Agamas, 300 books for a total of 3 million
words. These are classical texts, without paragraphs or punctua-
tion, so it was very difficult reading. It took me a year and a half
to read these 7.5 million words. That is because I also spent
much of my time in sitting meditation.

After I finished the sutras, I read from the extensive literature on the Chinese Chan tradition. The texts on Chan and the
eight different schools in Chinese Buddhism have a total of 7.5
million words. After I finished reading about Chan, I read the
history and biographies of Buddhism, a total of 600 books with
around 6 million words.

I wasn't reading the sutras for any particular personal benefit, other than to verify the experiences of my mind. I wanted
to organize Buddhist teachings so that they would be more accessible than they had been in the past. I believed that it had
been too long since someone had organized Buddhist literature. The history was long and there were many schools, so the
literature was too complicated for ordinary people to understand. I wrote both scholarly and popular books so that people

could understand that even though there are many sects of Buddhism, they are just different perspectives of the same Buddhadharma. The sects all share the same goal and foundation. I wanted to organize the Buddhadharma into an accessible system so that more people could understand it and apply it to their lives.

My meditation practice was also a big part of my six years of solitary retreat, but what happens in meditation should not be discussed. I don't even discuss this when I teach. I only teach people how to mediate. When something is described in words, it is already different from the experience itself. Some people experience hearing sounds or seeing visions. These are considered illusions, as mentioned numerous times in the sutras. It is normal to have these experiences in meditation practice.

The true principle or goals of the practice should be decreasing attachment and vexation and seeing the world positively, not focusing on contradictions and conflicts. When encountering contradictions and conflicts, one uses them positively. For example, I had lots of pests in my small room during the solitary retreat, but I didn't consider them a nuisance. My mind felt expansive and unrestricted by my physical environment.

When I saw animals looking for food in my room, I observed that stronger animals ate the weaker ones, and I understood that this is how nature works. I saw a frog eating flies and insects by darting its tongue out quickly. I thought: this is the way the animal world is; sentient beings are ignorant, the strong eat the weak, and probably a similar situation exists among humans. That's what Shakyamuni Buddha saw.

When the eagle eats the snake, does the human shoot the eagle? That would be ignorant. Compassion is mainly about not causing harm to sentient beings. We can't stop sentient beings from hurting each other because ignorance is part of our nature.

During these six years of retreat, life was very peaceful. I had some special experiences. I heard the sound of the ants and felt that I had floated off my cushion. My mind was very peaceful during my solitary retreat. I felt emotionally stable, with little fluctuation in my emotional state.

I see my meditation practice as distinct from my religious faith, and faith had been and would be an important part of my life. I had religious experiences based on faith when I encountered difficulty and recited Guanyin Bodhisattva's name. In the army, I recited Guanyin's name all the time. When I wanted to take the exam to qualify to become an officer, I had only had four years of elementary school. All the other candidates had been to college. But I had faith in Guanyin, and prayed to the bodhisattva, who helped me. The exam questions turned out to be the ones I had studied for. I didn't even have the qualifications to take the exam; still, I was allowed to take it. So I believe Guanyin Bodhisattva helped me.

It seemed impossible to leave the army because I worked in intelligence and was supposedly privy to secret and sensitive information. But I recited Guanyin Pusa's name, and I was eventually granted my freedom. When I wanted to go into solitary retreat, many old monks told me that it was impossible for someone who had just left the army to find a place to do so. But I believed in Guanyin, and I ended up with two or three options for my solitary retreat. I had many of these kinds of religious experiences.

I still feel that as long as I recite Guanyin's name, whatever problems I have will be resolved. That is why I never worry. People with strong religious faith often have this sense of security, willpower, and the courage and conviction to act in any given situation.

My meditation practice, which was distinct from these faith-based experiences, had helped to stabilize my mind and personality. In deep meditation, I have felt one with the universe. This is what Chan calls "unified mind." Self-centeredness disappears, but there still exists an idea of the universal self. The scope of one's mind is vast. As long as there is a sense of self, feeling at one with the universe is the highest possible accomplishment in meditation. You feel at one with God. Usually the most you can attain is unification with what is around us. I have had a lot of experiences of unification with the surrounding environment. Once I was touring with a group in Bangkok. While everyone was drinking coffee, I was looking at the fish in the river. Everyone found it strange that I was so interested in the fish, but I was in meditation, unified with the environment. When I looked at the fish, it felt as though I was right there in the water, gliding around with them. Illusionary phenomena can occur during meditation, but it is best not to pay too much attention. On my solitary retreat, I was meditating one evening. There was a clear sky and a full moon. But I heard heavy rain and wailing wind. I went out to check the sky, but it was clear. Another time when I was calmly meditating it sounded as if a tree behind my hut had come crashing to the ground. My mind was moved by the sound, and I went out to take a look. The tree, of course, was intact, but when I came back to meditate, I was distracted and unsettled.

Another time, when I was meditating, my body floated above the cushion. It was not an illusion, it really happened. I was very surprised and puzzled about why I was floating. Once my mind moved, I descended back to my cushion slowly. These were things that happened during meditation when I was in solitary retreat.

But the experiences of meditation, even at their most illuminating, mystical, and profound, are not enlightenment. "Seeing the nature," or enlightenment, is a completely different thing. Meditation cannot get one to see one's true nature. Religious experience is not enlightenment. Seeing one's nature is letting go of the mind, be it unified or not. There is no attachment whatsoever. Many people think that mystical experiences are the same as enlightenment. These experiences can come from meditation or religious experiences, but they are not enlightenment.

During my retreat, I woke in the morning and in a blink of an eye it was evening. Several people came to visit me, including Dongchu. I wrote several books during the retreat about the history of Buddhism, comparative religion, and Buddhism and Chan. I wanted to keep contributing to the world. It was just a time during which people could not disturb me, and I had time to read and write and practice.

A Survey of the Buddhist Vinaya and Precepts (Jieluxu gangyao) and the History of Indian Buddhism, which I wrote while I was on retreat, have been used as textbooks in mainland China since the end of the Cultural Revolution. Taiwanese universities have used The Study of Comparative Religion as a reference book. Orthodox Chinese Buddhism is a popular book among laypeople and has sold over three million copies around the world.

When I entered solitary retreat, Buddhism was in decline in mainland China and Taiwan. Few followers engaged in daily practice. Intellectuals considered Buddhism a superstition for uneducated people. Christianity was very popular. High level government officials in Taiwan were mostly Christians, although a few officials practiced Buddhism secretly.

I wrote critically, pointing out the problems of Buddhism in society. I knew only too well from my own experience that monasteries were supported by three means, which had nothing to do with teaching the Buddhadharma: performing rituals and reciting sutras for the deceased, accepting donations from tourists, and farming in the mountains (monks were essentially farmers, as this had always been their most successful means of support). No one taught or studied the Dharma. Most monastics were illiterate—and my essays criticized this phenomenon.

In the later part of my retreat, a layperson named Baiyi Yang, who was educated in Japan and had read my books and essays, would ride his motorcycle from Taibei to visit me. What a long trip it was for him, around 600 kilometers each way on dirt roads. Baiyi Yang was a great guy. Each time he came he brought over a dozen books that had been salvaged from people's trash. Many of them were on Japanese Buddhism.

I taught myself Japanese during the retreat and then read the books in Japanese. After reading these books, I stopped writing critical essays. Master Nanting inspired me to change course. He wrote to me, saying: "It's no use scolding people, the only useful thing is to stand up oneself." Master Dongchu also wrote, saying, "If you scold others now, you will receive retribution later."

Also, after I read the Japanese books Baiyi Yang brought, I was filled with hope. It was clear to me that Buddhist scholarship was alive and well in Japan. I learned that there were over five hundred doctoral students doing research on Buddhism in Japan, something that was unimaginable in China.

During the Meiji period (1868–1912), Japan's government,

like China's in the 1950s, set out to destroy Buddhism. Emperor Meiji forced monastics to eat meat, get married, and live in Shinto temples, and Shinto followers moved into Buddhist monasteries. As a result, Buddhism and Shintoism became indistinguishable. At the end of the Meiji period, Buddhism was revived. Many former Buddhist monastics returned to monasteries, but they kept their wives and continued to eat meat. That is how there came to be Buddhist monasteries where meat was eaten and wives lived.

These meat-eating married monks contributed greatly to Buddhist scholarship. They sent people to Germany and India who learned and did research in Sanskrit, and many famous Buddhist scholars emerged. I felt that if Buddhism in Japan had survived and flourished after being nearly completely obliterated, perhaps Buddhism in China could also be revived.

What really changed for me on retreat was how I thought about people. I started out being critical, both of humanity in general and particularly of how Buddhism had been corrupted in China. By the end of my retreat I stopped criticizing others. I realized that it is not effective to ask other people to change. Changing yourself is the only thing you can rely on.

During the last two years of my retreat, I corresponded with a former monk named Mantao Zhang who was studying in Japan. "After you are done living in the mountains, come to Japan and check it out here," he wrote. He described Buddhist activity in Japan and the rich scholarly climate there. "Just come and see how you like it. You don't have to stay."

Mantao was quite a fellow. He had no job and no money, but he did have a wife. He somehow managed to pay for his tuition and living expenses, because he was a very sociable person and loved to make friends. He met people willing to feed him and give him accommodations. He was unable to finish his doctorate degree, however, because his life was unstable.

When I did finally go to study in Japan, Mantao had returned to Taiwan. But it was because of his encouragement and information that I felt I should go to Japan.

Mantao was not the only person to urge me to go to study in Japan. "Come out of the retreat as soon as possible," Dongchu wrote me midway through my retreat. "Don't just live on the mountain. Young people nowadays should go abroad and study in Japan. I will pay all your expenses."

I didn't believe Dongchu could or would support my study in Japan. I am glad that I didn't fall for his trickery, insisting, instead, on staying in solitary retreat through the full term.

After my retreat ended, I went to Dongchu. "Shifu," I said, "I need to go to Japan. Please give me some support."

"I *had* planned to support your tuition and living expenses in Japan," he replied. "But you would not listen to me. Now my promise has been voided."

I then believed Dongchu wanted to trick me to leave my retreat early so that I could return to his place and continue to do work there. My younger Dharma brother had already left and my master was on his own. That was how I judged Dongchu's motives at the time, but I discovered later that it was not the case. He was studying Japanese writing and went to Japan later to collect data. He wrote a book titled *The History of Buddhist Exchange between China and Japan*. He saw Japan as very important. He had lived in Japan when he was young and could speak some Japanese. It made sense that he wanted me to study in Japan.

Later on, when *I* wanted to go to Japan, he said: "When I

told you to go to Japan, you didn't want to go. I can't help you now that you want to go." This was in accordance with the way Dongchu trained his students, encouraging us to be self-reliant. He was not saying that he did not support my going to Japan, only that I should find a way to go on my own.

Lampooned and Feared

Before I began my retreat, an old layperson visited me and asked, "What kind of monk do you want to be?" Because I was supposed to practice diligently while on retreat, people wondered how I would turn out afterward. It was as if they wanted to know how a piece of pottery would turn out after it had been fired in a kiln.

To live in solitude is excruciating for most Asians. Solitary confinement is the worst punishment in Asian penal systems, worse even than death. Monastics who survive long retreats are automatically assumed to have attained the Way; they are revered and viewed as extraordinary.

Whether or not they have indeed attained the Way, however, depends on what they actually do while they are on retreat. Some people become monastics because they don't know what they want to do with their lives. After they enter the monastic order, they are still unsure, so they decide to go on a solitary retreat, and they look for donors to sponsor them. I have seen some solitary retreat rooms with several hundred locks on the door; each

lock signifies a donor. These monastics spend all day reciting sutras for their donors' families. Three years spent reciting sutras
for others may lead to little improvement in oneself. It is a
pitiable state of affairs, although it is still quite a feat to spend
three years alone.

My retreat did not leave me hard-baked and definite, like a
piece of pottery. I did not decide to identify myself as a Dharma
master, a Chan master, or a Vinaya master, and I had not chosen
which of the four great masters to emulate. Would I be like Master Taixu, a reformer who advocated better standards for monks
and changes in the property ownership of monasteries? Would I
try to become another Master Yinguang, a Confucian thinker
who encouraged practice among laypeople? Or would I emulate
Master Hongyi, a former artist who strictly upheld the precepts
and wrote out his teachings in beautiful calligraphy? I could also
strive to be like Master Xuyun, who devoted himself to rebuild-
ing more than a dozen monasteries and was tortured by the
Communists as a subversive. Several times, he was beaten, it was
thought, to death. But he couldn't be put down and miraculously sprang back to life.

These great masters all died before I went on retreat, and I
felt that it was impossible for me to emulate them. I sought instead
to do my best to emulate Shakyamuni Buddha. On retreat, I came
to know what it was to experience a daily, living relationship with
him. I knew that I wanted to continue to learn from him, and I
didn't know which direction that would take me. What I would become and what I would do depended on the causes and conditions that would ripen in the future. Many people try to set goals
for themselves, such as making a certain amount of money, writing a certain number of books, and so on. These kinds of goals are
not reliable. In the future, your health and the environment you
live in will affect what you can actually accomplish.

A young monk I knew was a good writer and very intelligent. He published award-winning novels and political commentary. Many people thought that he was on the road to great renown. But his sangha bag was filled with photos of women.

"Why do you have so many pictures of women?" I asked him

"These women kept giving me their pictures," he said. "I don't want to be rude. So I keep them."

This was a monk who told himself he would surpass Master Taixu's accomplishments. And yet he ended up renouncing his vows and returning to lay life because he attracted so many women. The lesson of this, I think, is that we should not boast about what we will become in the future; instead, we should be clear about who we are right now.

I came out of solitary retreat at a time when Taiwan was a cultural and intellectual desert. There were only two newspapers on the entire island, both controlled by the government, and there were just a few literary magazines. Bookstores were rare. There was very little publishing going on; writers couldn't make a living. Art was taught in school, but very few people had the time to appreciate art or the money to spend on it. There were almost no professional artists, musicians, or dancers. The only thing left was sports on the radio. The sport teams were military, not civilian, because civilians barely had enough to eat. How could they possibly compete in sports? The only place with any cultural life was the military. Bored soldiers would perform plays. When a couple of movie stars visited Taiwan from Hong Kong, the entire island was mesmerized.

There was also considerable discrimination against monks. Although I was quite well-read and had published essays in popular magazines and newspapers, I was forbidden from entering a university. The belief was that a Buddhist monk could not be knowledgeable enough to participate in higher education. Intellectuals, educators, and high government officials in Taiwan all believed that Buddhism was for uneducated people, those in the lower strata of society. That is because Buddhists usually also engaged in folk religious practice. They worshipped gods and folk heroes. Temples were established to honor powerful spirits, and these temples also had Buddha and Daoist statues. Chinese people aren't very religious, particularly in the upper classes. The well-to-do who had been educated in the West sometimes became Protestant or Catholic. Although a minority, they became quite influential, connected to high-level government officials and other intellectuals. Buddhists had no such connections.

In fact, there were plenty of intellectual Buddhists; the native Taiwanese who had been educated in Japan and become Buddhists had difficulty getting into high-level positions because they mainly spoke Japanese, and most of the high-level officials in Taiwan were Nationalists from mainland China who spoke Mandarin.

I became a traveling teacher, holding classes and giving lectures wherever I could. I taught at Buddhist institutes in Gaoxiong City and Taibei. My books *History of Indian Buddhism, The Study of Comparative Religion,* and *A Survey of the Vinaya and Precepts* were all actually written for these institutes. I composed and compiled the material as I taught the classes and then turned the notes into books. At that time, not many people were writing textbooks. These books became very popular, and I went on to write many others, also based on my classroom lectures. As a result, I have published over one hundred books in both Chinese and English in my long life.

I taught my classes at these institutes and then left to teach elsewhere. I had informal conversations with my students. I taught them meditation and met them for tea. Older professors looked down on such fraternizing. They thought it was unethical to speak casually with students. When I was a student in the Buddhist institute, our teachers kept a great distance from us. We were really scared to talk to them, and we did not approach them without a good reason.

I was a controversial figure in other ways. I was well-known in Taiwan's small Buddhist circle from the articles that I had been publishing since I was in the army. I had made a name for myself by being critical of others. I was feared because I was unpredictable. No one knew what I would dare to write next. It was not that they feared that I would become more powerful than they were. I was feared because I had a reputation for scolding people in print. But I didn't criticize from malice. I wanted to get across new ideas.

I advocated modernizing Buddhism, making the Dharma useful in daily life. My critics didn't like it when I used modern language to explain the Dharma. For example, I advocated that monastics should use the Dharma to bless newly married couples, although monastics should not be matchmakers. I thought couples should be allowed to have their weddings in monasteries so they could learn to use the Dharma in their family life. Many people scolded me. They said, "Monasteries are pure places. Women shouldn't be allowed inside them. How can you advocate letting people get married in the monastery?" Many people still feel this way today. Because I criticized others so often, I felt it was right for others to criticize me. This is just retribution, I thought whenever I learned what people had to say about me. I was criticized in the classroom or in published essays—never to my face.

Another reason I was singled out was that I did not choose to follow a particular school of Buddhism. Taiwan's Buddhist circle was quite small, consisting of about a hundred people, and the groups were not very distinct or organized. They were more like social cliques, often organized around whether the people in them were mainlanders or native Taiwanese. I would participate in the groups and attend their activities, but I didn't socialize with them, and I didn't choose one over another. I didn't even join my master's group, because I didn't like socializing. I was a loner. When I was invited to a social gathering, I would always say: "I don't have the time."

Time was not the only reason I didn't want to attend. My retreat had set me apart. My practice and my relationship with Buddha were more important to me than parties. I also found that I had developed an increased sensitivity to what was around me. My intuition was heightened. I seemed to know when someone was talking about me. I knew when someone was coming to see me, even if he didn't have an appointment. I would sense this person was on his way, or think of him two or three times, and he would show up. When I asked him why he came, he would say, "I don't know. I just wanted to see you," or, "I dreamed of you and wanted to come see you." I also sensed when Master Dongchu wanted me to leave solitary retreat, and two days later I received his letter telling me that it was time to go. I would later sense the moment he passed away, even though I was living in the United States, thousands of miles away.

I'm not the only person with this level of intuition. Children sometimes feel that their mothers are thinking about them and respond by calling home. Practitioners are more likely to develop this level of intuition, though. I'm not talking about supernatural powers. People who have supernatural powers can hear and see whatever they want to hear and see. The Chan tradition avoids cultivating supernatural powers. Chan masters who happen to obtain supernatural powers through their practice don't talk about it, and they don't encourage others to develop such powers. Supernatural powers may seem useful, but even if you know something other people can't know, can you really improve their lives?

Many factors work to maintain balance in the universe. Even if you prevent something bad from happening by supernatural means, you are merely delaying the inevitable. The same causes and conditions would eventually arise in a different form.

Buddhist laws are very strict, prohibiting monastics from manifesting or using supernatural power. I don't want such power myself. When I feel it, I don't pay any attention. For example, sometimes I feel the presence of a local earth god or spirits living under a big tree or in a graveyard or shaded dark place. I don't worry about them. If I thought about them, I would cause myself unnecessary trouble. People might expect me to be a "ghost buster," checking out their homes to see if spirits are living there because they don't feel at peace, and I have no interest in that role.

13

In the Land of the Rising Sun

In 1969, at the age of thirty-nine, I traveled to Japan to attend Rissho University to pursue a doctoral degree in Buddhist literature. I attended Buddhist symposia and conferences, some of them international in scope. I listened to famous Buddhist scholars from all over the world.

There was a vibrant intellectual atmosphere outside the university as well. The Japanese people were generally interested in and knowledgeable about different religions. Newspapers and magazines published articles about religious activities. NHK, the public television channel in Japan, set aside a time slot for religious groups and for broadcasting religious symposia. In Taiwan, people may have been believers, but they had no education when it came to religious matters.

Japan was the first Asian nation to embrace Western culture. Whenever a new book was published in Europe, it would be translated into Japanese. Whenever a new technology came out, the Japanese would quickly master it. I felt that the air I breathed was the air of the world.

The Japanese were kind to tourists and students from other Asian countries. They did not bully outsiders, the way the Chinese did. When I got lost once in Tokyo, I asked for directions from a construction worker on the roadside. He wasn't sure that I understood him, so he took me himself to a bus station to help me get a ticket to get back to work. Once, someone even bought my ticket for me.

So much was different in Japan. Each home I visited was tidy and clean, as were the supermarkets, everything neatly arranged on shelves. The markets in Taiwan were dirty and chaotic. Japanese cuisine was also much less greasy than Taiwanese food and suited me better.

Japan's cultural and intellectual life was exciting. People read all the time on the subways and buses. Even common people—factory workers, small business owners—seemed well informed. The libraries and museums were excellent. The museums had artwork from China that was no longer available on the mainland or in Taiwan. Chinese people who wanted to study Chinese art had to go to Japan.

Democracy was alive in Japan in a way that was unimaginable in Taiwan. People criticized politicians and the government, sometimes harshly, in political cartoons, but they never criticized the emperor. Also, twice a year, in the spring and fall, students or workers would demonstrate on the street, blocking traffic. They wore bandanas around their foreheads and masks covering their faces, with only their eyes showing to protect their identities, fearing that participating in the demonstrations would jeopardize their standing at their school or job. Workers protested for the rights of minority groups or against certain government policies. The protests could be quite fierce. Police crackdowns sometimes led to violence. But Japanese society was not thrown into chaos by these demonstrations. The protests seemed useful, a part of democracy in action.

Traditional religion in Japan contained many ideas and rites brought from China that had been influenced by Japanese culture. Two obvious examples of this are Pure Land and Nichiren Shoshu, both Japanese-style Buddhist schools. They were different from the Buddhism that I saw in Taiwan, which was an outgrowth of the Buddhism that evolved during the Ming and Qing dynasties. Buddhism practiced in mainland China had roots that went back to before the Ming dynasty. In Japan, I saw the Buddhist practice from ancient China all the way to the contemporary period. In Nara and Kyoto, for example, the Buddhist monasteries followed the traditions established in the Tang dynasty. In Kamakura, near Tokyo, monasteries followed traditions from the Yuan dynasty.

There were also new schools of Buddhism: Soka Gakkai, Rissho Kosei-Kai, Reiyukai, and many small organizations run by laypeople. These schools advocated integrating Buddhist teachings into contemporary society. They ran youth groups, women's groups, and other groups based on age, with special activities geared toward their members. Traditional Buddhism didn't do that. The new schools proselytized like Christians, knocking on doors to try to get people to join them.

I enjoyed practicing with many different sects in Japan. I was curious about everything. I participated in several *sesshin* (intensive meditation retreats) at Zen monasteries. I did Nichiren Shu's retreat, reciting *Namu Myoho Renge Kyo* (Homage to the *Lotus Sutra*). I went on Tibetan Buddhist retreats and joined gatherings of other new Buddhist groups. Everywhere I went, people felt that I should join their group because I took to their practice so easily. But I still chose Zen in the end: I didn't need other ways of practice. I remember Bantetsugyu Roshi, a Zen abbot, with special gratitude. He was renowned for his stern style of Zen. I attended several winter retreats at his temple in Tohoku, which was in northern Japan. It was freezing in his temple during the winter, and he seemed inclined to give me an especially hard time. He ordered his assistants to constantly beat me. Of the people on these retreats, I had by far the most education. "You scholars have a lot of selfish attachments and vexations," he would say. "Your obstructions are heavy."

I was struck in Japan by how many different approaches there were to Buddhist practice. At one place, the *sesshin* were quite strict. But afterward everyone except the teacher pooled money to buy wine so they could relax after working so hard! I asked one of the participants, a monk, "Why do you need to drink wine after the *sesshin*?"

"I didn't become enlightened during *sesshin*," he replied. "Besides, this is not alcohol. We call it wisdom soup and perhaps I will become enlightened after drinking it!"

"Alcohol actually makes us ignorant," I said. "It's not going to enlighten you."

He laughed at me. "How do you know? You don't even drink. How can you be a man?"

One very cold winter, a classmate from Rissho University took me to Nichiren's main monastery for a retreat. The people who greeted me told me to take a look at what we would be doing. After breakfast, they rubbed their bodies with towels until their skin turned red. Then they doused themselves in cold water from the well. They gasped, crying, "Oh! Oh! Oh!" Steam rose from them. I knew that I could not engage in this kind of practice. I thought to myself, "This was not a method taught by Shakyamuni Buddha!" With my health, if I took off my clothes and poured cold water on myself, I would catch a cold for sure.

I did live there for several days, though, in a separate guesthouse for laypeople, and joined them for morning and evening services. When I visited these Zen monasteries to practice, they did not think of me as a monk.

I had a very strong experience with a Tibetan Buddhist group, which I joined once a week for sessions that ran from 8:00 A.M. to 5:00 P.M. This group practiced diligently, with a method that emphasized visualization. When I was concentrating deeply, my sense of self dissolved. I began to speak in a language I didn't understand. The participants said that I was speaking Sanskrit.

"That's what Sanskrit is like?" I asked, because I didn't think what I was saying sounded like Sanskrit.

"There are different ways of pronunciation in Sanskrit," they said. "You are chanting a Sanskrit mantra."

I stopped myself from thinking that this experience was strange, because I knew that by thinking it was strange I was rejecting it. I just let the mantras come out naturally. I found that different mantras came out of each practice session. Sometimes we practiced mudras—symbolic hand gestures—such as the Guanyin or Manjsuri. Sometimes the mantras were spoken. The mantras changed because they didn't come from my consciousness or will. Usually the mudras manifested first, followed by a mantra that I recited.

Many people had practiced the meditation method of their particular group for a long time and didn't have my type of experience. That's why the participants thought I should join their group and propagate their school of Buddhism. One of their monks took me to their monastery in Kyushu, very far away from where I was living in Tokyo. I stayed there several days. His father, mother, and girlfriend were all very nice to me. The monk told me many stories about life in his group. He wanted me to join them and spread the group's teachings in Taiwan. When I left Japan, he gave me a set of monk's clothes. I wasn't interested in joining his group, but I still cherish the set of robes he gave me.

Word got back to Taiwan that I was practicing with several different groups. My old colleagues were very worried that I was following some evil path. But I was very clear in my mind that was not the case.

After six years in Japan, I finished my doctorate. I wrote my dissertation on Master Ouyi Zhixu, who lived in the sixteenth century. He had a deep influence on me. Chan masters of his time were mostly skilled at smart talking, with many koans or verbal paradoxes. ("What is the sound of one hand clapping?" is a famous koan.) Zhixu criticized them severely for lacking in Buddhist practice and understanding. He advocated scholarly research and discourse. He held that if a Chan master does not understand Buddhist scholarship, he does not understand the teachings in Buddhadharma and cannot teach the Dharma to others. Similarly, if Chan masters do not understand the Vinayas and uphold the precepts, they cannot truly be Chan masters, because they do not live like practitioners.

He also felt Buddhist scholars must practice Chan and uphold the precepts. Without practice, a person cannot train his mind and resolve vexations. Though Zhixu had a deep influence on me, I still did not see myself as a master of Chan, or Vinaya, or Buddhist discourse. I was just a monk. I became whatever I needed to be, according to the causes and conditions of my life.

14

Forays West

When I was on solitary retreat, a Chinese immigrant in Toronto, Liwu Zhan, wrote to me, telling me that he really admired what I was doing. He asked if he could come have a cup of tea with me in the mountains.

I wasn't sure what he meant. "I welcome you to come to the mountain," I wrote back. "The tea here may be a bit flavorless. If you don't mind the lack of flavor, you can come."

"I have drunk your cup of tea. Thanks," he responded. He was referring to a Chan koan about Master Zhaozhou and drinking tea. When people asked him about the Dharma, he responded, "Drink tea."

People thought this advice had deep meaning. But there is nothing mysterious or deep about it. Chan is about daily life and being given what you need in each moment. In the mountains, when people visit, they get very thirsty from the trip, so they are told to drink tea to satisfy their thirst. The advice is nothing special. It's just about fulfilling a need.

Later, when I was in Japan, revising my dissertation for publication, Liwu Zhan wrote again. He asked what I planned to do when I finished my degree. He invited me to come to Canada. He wanted me to build a temple on eighty acres of land near Niagara Falls. He told me he would establish a professorship for me at Victoria College at the University of Toronto. This was a tremendous opportunity. I was very excited and accepted his invitation.

Dr. C. T. Shen (Shen Jiazhen), a cofounder of the Buddhist Association of the United States, helped me with a visa application to the United States. Shen was a banker from Shanghai who headed a trading company in Hong Kong. In the 1950s, he moved to the United States to start a shipping business, which was very successful. He had become interested in Buddhism in Hong Kong, and grew to be a major benefactor for Buddhist research and programs. He helped me with my studies in Japan, and we corresponded frequently during that time. He never held it over me that he was the person supporting my studies. He just showed sincere interest and compassion.

When I told him I planned to teach in Toronto, he suggested that I apply for a U.S. visa, which would make it easier for me to go to Canada, and sent me application forms. At the time, it was relatively easy for religious workers to get visas, and my application was quickly approved. After I published my dissertation, I left for America.

I arrived in New York in December 1975. I didn't go to Toronto until the following May. Mr. Zhan was not very happy about the delay. It turned out to be the first of many disappointments. Then he discovered that my English was poor. He had assumed that someone with an advanced degree would know the language. He realized that he would have to find someone to translate my lectures from Chinese into English at Victoria College.

I had disappointments of my own. I discovered that he planned to use only five of his eighty acres for the temple he had mentioned in his correspondence with me. After the temple was built, Liwu Zhan had the rest of the land earmarked for apartments. The temple was mainly meant to be a tourist attraction.

"Where is the money to build the temple going to come from?" I asked.

"You will have to find the money yourself," he said.

"I have no money and no followers."

"How dare you come here without money or followers!" he responded.

I didn't know what to say to that. He must have thought I was like Master Xuyun, who had people supporting him wherever he went. I had let him down, and I felt shamed. Later, I told a layperson that I had been tricked.

"You're a monk," he said. "Why can't you let this go?"

He was right. That layperson taught me Dharma.

I made a mistake, but there was no need for regret. I learned not to make the same mistake again.

My first lecture at Victoria College was about the similarities and differences of Chinese and Japanese Buddhism. This topic, apparently, did not interest scholars and students in Canada. Only one person who studied Asian religions was intrigued, and he urged people to attend the lecture.

C. T. Shen found an interpreter who was Chinese and worked at the United Nations. His English was excellent. But he didn't know much about Buddhism. He was not familiar with the names and locations I mentioned in China and Japan. The audience was confused since most of them were faculty and students interested in Asian studies and knew when the interpreter misconstrued.

"You should have given me the lecture notes beforehand," the interpreter said. He was fuming after the lecture.

"Aren't you a simultaneous interpreter at the U.N.?" I asked.

"At the U.N., I only do simultaneous interpretation in my specialty subjects. When I'm interpreting for other subjects, I need to be able to prepare beforehand."

Failure after failure plagued me in Canada. I realized that it would not be possible for me to stay at the university as a professor. I lectured at Victoria College one more time and left. The whole plan was off: the seminar series, the plan to build a temple on Mr. Zhan's land, and all his efforts to win support for the project. I felt that I had to face reality. Failure is failure. It had taken courage on my part to come all the way to Canada, but it made sense that I failed because the conditions for my success were not in place. I was so naïve, and did not think everything through beforehand. Guts were not enough. But I am grateful for the opportunity Mr. Zhan gave me. If I hadn't had the invitation to go to Canada, C. T. Shen might not have invited me to the United States.

I decided to accept Shen's invitation to live at the Temple of Great Enlightenment in the Bronx, New York. I still had my visa and was able to reenter the United States. Otherwise, I would have had to go back to Japan to teach. I did not want to return to Taiwan. I had the reputation there as a wandering monk, and a controversial wanderer at that. Once I left to study in Japan, the monasteries in Taiwan did not want me to return. They were content with the way things were in Taiwan's Buddhist circles.

As I planned my move to New York, I realized that what I wanted to do was to devote my life to teaching Chan Buddhism. I made this decision because based on what I read and what people who had been to America had told me, I knew that Buddhism in the West emphasized what is applicable in daily life. By the 1950s, the writings and teachings of D. T. Suzuki on Zen had become very influential in the West. Americans wanted Buddhist meditation teachers, but it did not seem that Westerners were particularly interested in Buddhist discourse. So I became a Chan master, because Chan emphasized practices for daily life. In America, the books I would write and the lectures I would give all revolved around Chan. But among the books I've published in Chinese, Chan is only one of many subjects I have pursued. In Chinese society, I am known as a *fa shi* Dharma teacher.

I did not struggle with the decision to commit myself to teaching Chan Buddhism in America. The first monastery I was ordained in was Chan. Although I had conducted research in several Buddhist schools of thought, it was always from the perspective of a Chan master, seeking to understand how those texts could help with Chan practice.

Scholars who master the theories of the different schools of Buddhism without knowing Chan can never be more than academic Buddhists, without much influence. Why? Because their minds won't be clear. They won't be able to let go of the self, and they will remain attached to their own points of view. They won't be able to tolerate people with different perspectives.

Those who know Chan can tolerate everyone. When they see others, they see them as no different from themselves. They can accept everyone and can adapt to any environment. They don't have a doctrinaire idea of what Chan is. They can't go around saying, "This is Chan. That is not Chan." In Chan tradition, nothing sets Chan apart from anything else. Some Buddhists will use the phrase "non-Buddhist path," but in Chan there is really no such thing. All boundaries and barriers are transcended. I don't see followers of other religions as any different from me. When I eat, they eat. When I sleep, they sleep. There's no distinction

Eating Bitter

To become a great Chan master, one must start from very poor material conditions and work hard. Wolf Mountain, the monastery where I first became a monk, was very wealthy, with many patrons. But young monks ordained in the monastery trained for three years, doing homemaker's work. Everything a homemaker needs to do monks must be able to do: clean the house, grow vegetables, sew clothes and shoes, and cook food. The only thing they don't need to learn is how to bear a child. The goal was to train monks to get rid of their pride and not look down on those who engage in manual labor. Monks also need to be prepared to go to places where there are no followers, as Western missionaries do, and there they will need to know how to manage all the housework on their own. Manual labor is also a way to help students settle their minds, eliminating wandering, judgmental, or self-centered thoughts. Monastic life is difficult if you are always thinking about your own loss and gain, your own self. If you can't quiet your mind, you will suffer. Monastic life is simple with a mind of equanimity.

There are many great stories in the Chan canon of monks who must "eat bitter," or endure difficult menial work as they train. A story from the Tang dynasty of the ninth century tells of a young disciple who came to study Dharma with Master Bird Nest (the nickname of Master Daolin, which literally translates as "Path-forest"). The master lived in a tree, and the disciple lived on the ground, bringing him water and running errands for him. The disciple planned to learn Chan from the master in order to attain enlightenment. For six years, the master didn't teach him any Dharma. He just asked him to run errands. The attendant was crestfallen, and one day he told the master that he had to leave.

"Why do you have to leave?" the master asked.

"I came here to learn the Dharma," the disciple replied. "I have only been running errands. I have not learned any Dharma, which I need to attain enlightenment. So I am going to leave to find another learned friend who will teach me what I need to know."

"Ah, Dharma," said the master. "I have a little bit here." The master slowly pulled a loose thread from his robe and blew it into the wind. At that instant, his disciple experienced enlightenment.

The board members at the Temple of Great Enlightenment considered the lesson of this story as they prepared to welcome me. They knew I had just finished a doctorate and worried that I might be full of pride and would be haughty. They wanted to make sure that I had the chance to "eat bitter."

I didn't think that this was necessary. After all, I had been trained to eat bitter since I was a child. Perhaps they did not take this into account. When I arrived at the temple, they treated me as an ordinary monk rather than a *fa shi*, a Dharma master. They had me scour the monastery clean and rearrange all its rooms. I cleared out the basement, which was filled with junk, and turned it into a classroom and library. I turned the backyard into a nice garden with my bare hands.

I had no assistant and had to do everything myself. The other monks living there were older than I was. They were senior monks and did not offer to help me. When a truckload of books was shipped from Japan, I took care of getting them from the wharf to the monastery and arranged them in the basement library. I was used to working on my own after all my years in solitary retreat.

My surroundings were humble. At that time, that part of the Bronx was full of ramshackle homes and vacant tenements. The people in the neighborhood tended to be a mix of poor Latinos and Jews. There were very few Chinese. The area was mainly industrial and commercial. The monastery was a converted post office warehouse, which C. T. Shen had purchased. When I arrived, there were no bedrooms, and I slept in the basement, a dark, windowless, humid room. It was like living in a cave. I made an opening in the wall to let in some light and air.

The other monks were better off. They lived in rental apartments nearby. I was the only one living in the monastery itself. I was not asked to give lectures; I had no authority to make decisions, manage people, or take care of money matters. I had to live at the monastery to welcome visitors. So I was essentially a doorman.

The schedule at TGE was familiar. As a Chinese monastic, wherever you are, your daily routine is always the same. I got up at 4:00 or 5:00 A.M. for the morning service, had breakfast, and cleaned up. If I had English class, I went. If not, I tidied up the basement. If there were visitors, I took care of them. If I was tired, I took a rest. Because it was not a big organization, my schedule was flexible. After lunch, I rested and took care of the building and grounds. I was often alone; very few people came during the day to worship. If I had time, I did sitting meditation. I held evening service early, around 5:00 P.M., and then had dinner. Evenings, I showered, wrote, and did prostrations and sitting meditation. On Saturday mornings I taught meditation class to a small group of Western and Chinese immigrant students. Saturday afternoons I prepared the monastery for the Sunday lecture, which was given by a senior monk. I had to sweep indoors and out.

As the only monk living at the monastery, I did all the work except for the administrative duties, which were taken care of by Rev. Ri-chang Fa Shi, whose English was better than mine. I considered the housekeeping exercise and a kind of practice. It did not bother me.

Thanks to C. T. Shen, I did not have to "eat bitter" for long. He nominated me to serve as a board member and vice president of the Buddhist Association of the United States. Then he made me the abbot of TGE. I hadn't even been at TGE for half a year, so this was very special treatment. I don't think other monastics were treated as well.

At TGE, it was not a problem at first that I could not speak English. When I arrived, the participants were mostly Chinese. Occasionally, curious Westerners would come by, but they weren't quite sure what to do. They felt like they were in another country, especially since we were all speaking in Chinese. If the Chinese people there saw a Westerner, they would say, "A foreigner has come." I often reminded my fellow monastics that *we* were the foreigners and they were the natives!

I knew that I wanted to reach out to Westerners. I found myself recalling the advice of Bantetsugyu Roshi, one of my Zen teachers in Japan. "Zen is not taught with words," he told me when I expressed worries about the language barrier that I would face in America.

That advice helped me, even after my lack of English had been such a problem in Toronto. In New York, I taught Chan meditation; I was not expected to lecture to scholars and students. Chan's emphasis is to get directly to the heart of things. Using words to do this is like scratching an itchy foot with your shoes on. The goal is to guide students to their own realization of Chan. It is up to the student to realize his or her true mind, apart from words and language.

A disciple of Dazhu Huihai, a great master in Chan history, once asked him, "Can you teach me how to practice?"

He responded, "When I am hungry, I eat. When I am tired, I sleep. Words are not needed."

We should not think that Chan practitioners have lots of secrets, that what they do is so mysterious. They just live their lives in earnest, nothing complicated, without thinking about it much. Anyone can live this way.

I thought of how Bodhidharma did not speak Chinese when he went to China. I also recalled the story of the monk who had said to Master Zhaozhou: "I am very confused. Would the master please give me some guidance?"

Zhaozhou just said, "Have you had your rice soup already?"

The student answered that he had.

"Then go wash your bowl," Zhaozhou said. The student attained enlightenment in that moment.

So when I first started interacting with Westerners, I took a similar tack. If a student asked me for help, I asked in return, "Have you had dinner?"

If he said yes, I told him, "Then go wash your dishes."

I often chatted with my students this way, especially if a

translator wasn't around. I was not able to express much Dharma in English, so I kept things very simple. When a student asked, "What is the reason?" I would say, "No reason." They seemed to understand. Once a person in an elevator asked me, "Master, what is true reality?" I said, "There is no such thing." "Great!" he replied.

What I was able to express seemed to be enough to answer lots of questions. But C. T. Shen was very concerned that I knew so little English. He said it would be inconvenient for me to stay in America without learning the language. He paid for a private tutor and classes. Because I was getting old, almost fifty, it was tough to learn the language. My memory was not as sharp as it had been when I was younger. After more than three hundred hours of costly lessons, I stopped. I was getting too busy and felt it was too expensive. C. T. Shen said he respected my decision, and helped me find a less intensive weekly class.

One day two young men, Franklin and Peter, came to the monastery and asked me if I knew kung fu.

"Yes," I said.

"What do you know?" they asked.

"I know Taiji and Shaolin."

Then I warned them that I did not teach bodily movement, the kind of kung fu shown in movies. "I teach the use of the mind," I said. "You first learn how to train your thoughts and stabilize your mind so that you don't get hurt by others."

"That sounds great," they said.

They brought several friends with them to the first classes. I had no idea how to teach them at first, especially since I couldn't really teach in English. I was worried they would lose interest, but I moved forward with the class anyway. I asked a student of mine, Ming-yee Wang, to help me translate. He was a graduate student in mathematics at New York University, but he suffered from severe headaches. After he studied meditation with me, the headaches subsided.

Our meditation class met on Saturday mornings till early afternoon. We met once a week for four hours. At first, I had no idea how to use the time. I approached Rev. Ri-chang, whom C. T. Shen had sent to study with Philip Kapleau Roshi at the Rochester Zen Center in upstate New York.

"I have practiced in China and Japan in various monasteries, but I don't know what to teach in the West," I told Rev. Ri-chang. "What do they do at Kapleau's place?"

"It's very simple," he said. "They teach counting the breath. When a student can count his breathing well, with a calm mind, then they investigate koans."

I asked Rev. Ri-chang to help me teach. He was reluctant at first. We talked a little about Kapleau, who had become a famous American teacher of Zen. His master was Yasutani Roshi.

"Who is Yasutani's master?" I asked.

"Yasutani's master was Harada Sogaku," he said.

I told him that Sogaku was also the master of my master in Japan, Bantetsugyu. What this meant was that I was a Dharma brother of Kapleau Roshi, since we were both descendents from Harada. This led me to realize I would know how to teach Western students. Rev. Ri-chang was very happy to learn this and agreed to assist me.

We first taught our students the breath-counting method, as Rev. Ri-chang suggested. We kept the rest of the classes just as simple. I gave the students only a few sentences of direction, then I was done. I did not have a syllabus or a fixed lesson plan.

By the end of the three-month class only a few students remained. They were diligent and responded well to the concepts and theory introduced in the class. They felt they had found their teacher in me.

Frank told me that he planned to attend a kung fu competition in Central Park. "Shifu," he asked me, "when I am competing, could you please sit on the side? I will introduce you to everyone as my master. People will think that with my master at my side, I will win without having to fight."

I was really amused. "What if you lose and then they want to fight me?" I asked.

"No one will dare to challenge you," he said.

I smiled. "The highest level of martial art does not use weapons or gestures," I said. "When the other person attacks you, you must lose your sense of self. Then your opponent will not know how to attack you. Why? Because they will not know where to attack you. This is the teaching of no-self, no-mind. Whenever you have a self, when you try to attack or defend yourself, your opponent will be able to detect the weak spot in your defenses and exploit it. If you don't have a self, if you don't have anything to defend or any place to attack from, then there is no such weakness for your opponent to detect and exploit."

Frank and his friends listened intently. They vowed to practice so that they could attain this level.

"To accomplish this, you need to perfect your Chan practice first," I told them.

Some of my early students, accomplished martial artists, were training to become police officers. I was excited by how sincere they were and felt a great sense of accomplishment. They learned with a pure and innocent heart. I taught them in turn with a sincere heart, and they took everything in. As a result, the class was very effective.

I became the first Chan master to teach Chan to Westerners

on the East Coast. The only other Chan Master teaching West-erners was Master Xuanhua (Hsuan Hua), who founded the City of Ten Thousand Buddhas in California, one of the first Bud-dhist monasteries in the United States. He mainly taught ascetic practices: sleeping sitting up and fasting for one to three months. His approach was very popular among Westerners, and he had many Western disciples. Because his method of practice was a little eclectic, he was not considered part of the Chan com-munity in the United States at first. He was thought of as part of the Pure Land School, because he also taught the recitation of the Buddha's name.

In New York, most of the interest in Buddhism was in Japa-nese Zen and Tibetan Buddhism. In the Zen community, Shun-ryu Suzuki on the West Coast and Eido Shimano on the East Coast were well-known, active teachers. Taizan Maezumi, the founder of the Zen Center of Los Angeles, was also prominent. The Dalai Lama had already been to the United States a number of times, speaking about Tibetan tradition, and the Naropa Insti-tute of Chogyam Trungpa had opened in Denver, Colorado. The Sixteenth Karmapa, then head of the Tibetan Gelug sect, had vis-ited the United States. There was a small group of practitioners from the Pure Land School from Japan and some followers of the Korean master Seung Sahn. I interacted with many of these groups, because C. T. Shen supported all schools of Buddhism and invited masters from different schools to TGE to give lec-tures.

Chinese monastics, at that time, were concentrated in Chi-natown and did not teach Westerners or speak English. They were from mainland China, Hong Kong, Vietnam, Burma, and Taiwan. There were scattered around a dozen monasteries in Chinatown. The monks were not willing to break out of the Chinese community. The Zen masters, on the other hand—

Maezumi, Suzuki, and others—all spoke English very well. D. T. Suzuki had set a very strong foundation for Zen in America prior to these masters.

There is a long history behind Chan's relative isolation from the world. After the Song dynasty (960–1270 C.E.), Japan no longer sent any monks to China to study. In the Yuan and Ming dynasties (1368–1644 C.E.), Chinese Buddhism began its decline. Later on, during the Qing dynasty (1644–1911 C.E.), the emperor followed Tibetan Buddhism, thus precipitating the decline of Chinese Buddhism. The Japanese Buddhist scholars pronounced that there were no longer any Chan masters in China. That was not true. No one knew about the Chan masters because they were not able to attract students from abroad to study with them. Also, there was little training for young people in Buddhism. During World War II, there was no formal education for training young monks. After 1949, there was no Buddhism in mainland China. Conversely, in Japan, there was a very good educational system for Zen that was not disrupted by the war. Tibetan Buddhism also had a good training system. All this was lacking in Chinese Buddhism. That is why I eventually established a graduate school for Buddhist studies in Taiwan.

I have been asked whether Chan was less popular in the West than other forms of Buddhism because it is so integrated with Chinese culture. I don't think that's the reason. Japanese Zen is integrated into Japanese culture. Similarly, Tibetan Buddhism is integrated into Tibetan culture. I think the main reason that Chan is not more widespread is that there have been so few teachers who have come to the West.

I used the fact that I had been invited to teach in the United States as an opportunity. In 1977, I began to publish *Chan Magazine*, which eventually became a quarterly mailed out to more than fifty countries. But I didn't consider myself on a mission to propagate Buddhism. Rather I wanted to share Chan with everyone in the world. I believed if more people in the English-speaking countries accepted the method and concepts of Chan, they would have a beneficent influence on the rest of the world. They don't necessarily have to become Buddhist. As long as they practiced Chan in their daily life, they would be able to live happily, regardless of health or circumstances.

Wandering

As it turned out, Dongchu was not through with me just yet. Just when I had begun to get settled in my new secure role as abbot of the Temple of Great Enlightenment, he came to New York. This was in 1976, and he was very pleased to observe me teaching twenty Western students and decided that I would be the best choice to inherit Nongchan (Farming-Chan), his monastery in Taiwan, after he died.

"Taking over this monastery is like making wine," Dongchu said. "What I am giving you is the yeast to start the fermentation process. So don't think that my little monastery Nongchan is too small for you. If you do a good job, and start making wine successfully, you will be able to continue making wine for a long time to come."

Chinese people make wine with some fermented rice, wheat, or sorghum from a previous batch of wine to start the fermentation process. Dongchu was trying to tell me that Nongchan was like that portion of fermented grain.

"Don't worry," I told him. "I will take good care of the place."

Dongchu passed away soon after this visit, in fact so soon after that I had been abbot at TGE for only six months. I had a promising future in the Bronx, but I had to accept Dongchu's bequest. It was my inheritance. My master had sent me on a mission, and I had no choice in the matter: I had to pack up and go.

This sense of mission has a long history in Chan. Master Mazu sent more than a hundred disciples out in different directions to pass on the Dharma. They established monasteries by excavating mountainsides with their bare hands. It took them decades to build monasteries that were often very simple structures. As more practitioners came, the monasteries expanded. The purpose of establishing monasteries was not to have grand palaces to show off but to fulfill the responsibility of passing on the Dharma to future generations. The result of their efforts was that Chan masters throughout history had places of their own to practice.

Dharma transmission, passing on the responsibility of teaching the Dharma to future generations, started in Shakyamuni Buddha's time. This kind of inheritance is not as simple as passing on a crown. Some people who have experienced enlightenment may not be chosen to transmit the Dharma. They may not possess enough merit or skill. Chan tradition has strong emphasis on lineage transmission. The *Record of the Transmission of the Lamp*, compiled during the Jingde era (ca. 1004), recounts stories of the responsibility masters have to preserve and spread the Dharma to their heirs. This process, Dharma transmission, is what the "Transmission of the Lamp" refers to. Lineage transmission has occurred in Buddhism since the time of Shakyamuni Buddha.

So when my master gave me my inheritance, I embraced it. If I had refused, I would no longer have been Dongchu's disciple, and I would have disrupted the lineage of which I was a part and he had entrusted to me. A son can refuse an inheritance from his father, but it is a sacred tradition in Chan that a disciple cannot refuse to undertake a mission given to him by his master.

Master Dongchu, I should make clear, did not exactly *give* me Nongchan Monastery. The monastery's ownership belonged to a board of directors, not to me. What he gave me was a mission to pass on the Dharma, through overseeing the future of Nongchan.

I did not have to carve a monastery out of a mountain, but sometimes the task of helping Nongchan grow seemed that difficult. By giving up my position as abbot of TGE to go back to Taiwan, I was moving from a position of strength to one of weakness. TGE had the support of C. T. Shen's vast wealth and connections, and I never needed to worry about money there. When my Western followers in the United States learned that I would be going to Taibei to take over Nongchan, some asked: "Why are you leaving a place like TGE, which is ready-made for spreading the Dharma, to go to Taiwan to work so hard?" How could I explain to them the absolute obligation we Chinese feel about such things? I really had no choice in the matter.

When I returned to Taiwan, difficulties started right away. I discovered that Dongchu had left three different versions of his will. Chan masters typically do not leave wills. But Dongchu needed a way to express his wishes because I was not by his side during his last days. If I had been there, he would only have had to tell me that he wanted me to serve Nongchan in his place.

My name was not on the first two versions of his will because

I had told him twice that I would not be returning to Taiwan, once while I was studying in Japan and the second time right after I arrived in the United States. But after he visited me at TGE, and we agreed I would take over the running of Nongchan, he added my name to his last will.

The three versions caused much confusion among Nongchan's board members and followers. There was another monk involved, whom several influential people connected to Nongchan perceived as the heir, but I knew Dongchu did not want to entrust the mission to him. I had come all the way back to Taiwan, abandoning a secure position in the United States, only to find myself in the midst of controversy, chaos, and confusion. It was as if Dongchu had sent me on yet another contradictory errand. "Ho, ho, ho." Sometimes I thought I heard his ghastly laugh riding on the wind. After some months, thankfully, the other monk ended up leaving Nongchan, and my authority was no longer in dispute.

Nongchan was set on the outskirts of Taibei, in a rural area with farmland and small clusters of homes. The mountains that formed the spine of the island rose up behind it. The monastery itself was very small, with only a few followers and not enough money for groceries. I had to find volunteers to work at Nongchan and ways to raise money. Without more people to give time, energy, and money, the monastery would continue as a marginal operation, and Dongchu's vision of it as a secure, expanding base from which to propagate the Dharma would never be realized.

I set about attracting followers through meditation classes and retreats, using the teaching methods that I had developed in the United States. In the beginning, I taught mainly college students, and the retreats were only big enough for about twenty people, but they spread the word to others, which attracted more young people to the organization. Some of my students from those early days have become monastics who now occupy important positions in my organization. Some who remained in lay life have become important donors to Nongchan and the other monasteries and institutes that I established in the United States, Europe, and Taiwan.

To accommodate the increasing number of people at Nongchan, I had to do as Master Mazu's Dharma heirs did, and I expanded the monastery, adding to the building, sometimes illegally, with windows that were not up to code. The Taibei government wanted to tear the monastery down, but we avoided that fate because we contributed to the welfare of Taibei by holding large charitable events.

Dongchu had told me to advance Chan education in addition to spreading Chan practice at the monastery. When I first lived in Taiwan, there were no institutions to train young people in Buddhist education. That is why I went to Japan for my doctorate. My degree was useless in Taiwan: Taiwanese Buddhists didn't know what to do with someone with a doctorate in Buddhist literature. The system was very different in Japan. They sent outstanding people to study in India, Germany, and England. Each Buddhist sect created positions for these scholars when they returned to Japan, and they developed university-level educational programs.

I vowed to change the conditions in Taiwan by establishing institutions for training young people in Buddhist education. In 1978 I accepted an appointment as a professor at the Graduate School for Philosophy and as director of the Graduate Institute for Buddhist Studies at the Chinese Culture University. I also taught at Dongwu University. My courses were on Huayan, Tiantai, Pure Land, Madhyamika (Middle Way), Yogacara, (Consciousness-Only), and Chan. These appointments gave me a foothold in the educational system, and I was able to start a graduate institute of Buddhist studies. In 1985, I resigned from my position at Chinese Culture University and established the Chunghwa Institute of Buddhist Studies in Beitou. Now there are more than a dozen such institutes on the island.

After I arrived in Taiwan to accept my master's inheritance, I kept in close touch with C. T. Shen. When the president of the Institute of Sutra Translation, which he supported, resigned, I became president and the institute moved to Nongchan. Shen paid my salary.

But back in the United States, TGE needed help. After I left, there was a gradual attrition of monks until there was no one in charge of the monastery. Shen was eager that I return to the Bronx, resume my role there as abbot, and resuscitate the place. I felt an obligation to him to do so, but I could not tell him when I might be free of the responsibilities at Nongchan, which were too great for me to consider leaving.

Shen learned about an old nun who had escaped from mainland China through Burma and come to the United States. She didn't have monastery of her own, and Shen invited her and the entourage of nuns who had traveled with her to TGE. Around this time I was finally able to resign my post as the monastery's abbot.

After I finally managed to get Dongchu's affairs in order, C. T. Shen brought me back to New York to spread the Dharma there. My return to the United States did not restore me to my former position of strength, however. There was no room for me to live at TGE, which was occupied by nuns. I stayed at Shen's villa, named Bodhi House, on Long Island and traveled back and forth to the city. But I wanted to move out because I was too far away from my students. Shen told me, "If you move out, I can no longer take good care of you."

"That's okay," I said. "I will wander."

I had no money for rent, so I slept in front of churches or in parks. I learned how to get by from three of my students, who had experience living on the street. They taught me to find discarded fruit and bread in back of convenience stores and food markets. They showed me that I could make a little money here and there from odd jobs, sweeping up shops or tending a pretzel stand. I learned that I could store my things at a locker at Grand Central Terminal and wash clothes at a Laundromat. My students pointed out the fast-food restaurants that were open twenty-four hours, and they told me that I could spend my nights at these places, resting and drinking coffee.

I wandered through the city, a monk in old robes, sleeping in doorways, nodding with the homeless through the night in coffee shops, foraging through dumpsters for fruit and vegetables. I was in my early fifties, no spring chicken, but I was lit from within by my mission to bring the Dharma to the West. Besides, what did it matter? The lessons Dongchu had taught me made it a matter of indifference to me whether I slept in a big room or a small room or in the doorway of a church.

Some people may have felt pity for me, but I didn't pity myself. I didn't feel that I was unlucky. Some people feared me and worried that I would ask for money or other help. I decided it was best not to call on anyone, although I did accept some offers of help. I spent nights at the apartments of my followers. Master Haolin welcomed me and let me stay at his monastery in Chinatown. But I did not want to stay there too long because I did not know if I would be able to repay him for this service. I preferred to wander.

This may strike some of you as strange—that a friend and fellow monk would let me leave his monastery to live out on the street. But Haolin had a very small place without much income. When I lived there, it was an added burden on him. If he was wealthy and had a big place I would have felt differently about imposing on his hospitality.

I think that being out on the streets was a good thing, because it taught me not to rely on anyone and pushed me to find my own place to propagate Chan. There is a long tradition of bodhisattvas enduring difficulties as they spread the Dharma. Shakyamuni Buddha taught that to be a great practitioner, a bodhisattva, you do not look toward your own happiness and security. You only wish for sentient beings to cease suffering. In India, Buddhist monks had to travel to areas without Buddhism and they would inevitably encounter resistance. When they arrived in China, Confucianism and Taoism were dominant, and the Confucians wanted to keep the Buddhists out, especially the monastics. Shakyamuni Buddha believed that if you could withstand difficulties, you would be able to inspire others and thus influence them. Ordinary people just want life to be smooth, without problems. But Buddhist practitioners have a different attitude. They are ready to endure many difficulties if they are in the service of transforming others.

How do we endure hardship? Master Mazu taught that it is necessary to have a mind of equanimity. This means always maintaining a calm, stable mind, which is not ruled by emotion. When you encounter success, you don't think that *you* created it. Don't get too excited or proud of yourself. Your success happened for a reason and came to pass because of many people and circumstances. If you work hard at something, but find that too many obstacles prevent you from accomplishing it, you may have to give up. In that case, you shouldn't get depressed. Conditions aren't right. Perhaps this will change, perhaps it won't. *You* are not a failure. Becoming upset only causes suffering.

Keeping a mind of equanimity, though, does not mean being inactive or passive. You still need to fulfill your responsibilities. Master Xuyun said, "While the business of spreading Buddha's teachings is like flowers in the sky, we ought to conduct them at all times. Although places for the practice [monasteries, retreat centers] are like the reflection of the moon in the water [referring to the fact that they are illusory and impermanent], we establish them wherever we go." This means that these jobs are illusory, but we still need to do them. Sentient beings are illusory, but we still need to help deliver them. A place of practice is like the reflection of the moon in the water. It's not real, but we still build monasteries so we can deliver sentient beings. This is our responsibility. We must try our best to fulfill our responsibilities, without being attached to success and failure.

Chan masters apply the mind of equanimity in all aspects of their lives. If they don't, they are not truly Chan masters. In my time of wandering, I kept a mind of equanimity. I didn't think of myself as homeless. I thought of Master Hanshan, who lived on Tiantai Mountain. He used the sky as his roof, the earth as his bed, the clouds as covers, a rock as a pillow, and the stream as his bathtub. He ate vegetables if vegetables were available. If rice and vegetables were available in a monastery, he ate that. If nothing was available, he ate tree leaves or roots. He felt free and wrote beautiful poems.

> *Beneath high cliffs I live alone*
> *swirling clouds swirl all day*
> *inside my hut it might be dim*
> *but in my mind I hear no noise*

I passed through a golden gate in a dream
my spirit returned when I crossed a stone bridge
I left behind what weighed me down
my dipper on a branch click clack

When you have nothing, you are free. When you own something, then you are bound by your possessions. I felt very happy. I did not feel that I had no future. In fact I felt my future was rich and great indeed because I had students. I still had a mission to fulfill. I just did not know where I would sleep at night. I knew that I was much better off than homeless people, who really did not have anything and were without a future. And I knew that I would not wander forever.

My life is very different now. I have met with world leaders and given a keynote address in the general assembly hall at the United Nations. My disciples include high-level officials in Taiwan. I was received as a VIP in motorcades in mainland China and Thailand. I am venerated by my followers. People feel that if they don't treat me this way, it's not right, but it does not make any difference to me whether they treat me this way or not. I am famous today but tomorrow, when I can no longer do what I do now, I will be forgotten. How many people have their names remembered in history? Fame, like wealth and power, is illusionary. So a mind of equanimity is necessary in all circumstances.

There is a Chinese saying that goes: "After experiencing wealth and property, it is hard to return to poverty." This is true if you don't have a mind of equanimity. If you can maintain a mind of equanimity, you are free, no matter what the conditions.

The First Altar

In the time of my wandering, C. T. Shen continued to take care of me whenever possible. Shen owned a vacation home in Port Jefferson, on the north shore of Long Island, and it was called Bodhi House. Shen did not live there full time but used it as a personal retreat as well as a place to hold meetings and conferences. He graciously offered me this place to conduct retreats for my students. But the people who were involved in running and maintaining Bodhi House were very cold to me. They felt I had betrayed the Buddhist Association of the United States and the Temple of Great Enlightenment by returning to Taiwan to become the abbot of Nongchan. How could I explain that I did not do it on purpose, that my master passed away and I had no choice in the matter?

In the last retreat that I held at the Bodhi House, one of the participants arrived late, and opened the gate himself. When the caretaker discovered the gate open the next day, he pointed a gun at me. "You are all thieves!" he shouted. "I'll shoot you if it happens again."

I later told Shen, "We were at fault, but there was no need to point a gun at us."

"This person is really creating bad karma," he replied. He later sold Bodhi House.

There were other instances when I brushed up against the same attitude. I once tried to borrow some cushions from TGE, which I had made myself when I lived there. The nun in charge would not see me. She sent a disciple instead, who told me, "It's not convenient to lend you the cushions."

"Are you using the cushions?" I asked.

"That's our business," she said. This time, I didn't say anything to Shen.

So what did I do to find cushions? A homeless guy I knew had a friend who was a seamstress. She was also very poor and lived in a tiny apartment. She had a sewing machine and volunteered to sew the cushions for us for free, if we provided fabric and filling.

Until this point I had always thought: "To leave home is to be without home and everywhere can be home. There is no need to have my own place." But now I realized that in order to truly spread the Dharma and train practitioners well, I needed my own place. So, as it turned out, this nun did a wonderful deed by refusing to lend me the cushions.

When I was wandering around homeless for six months, it was winter and I greatly enjoyed my freedom. The city was windy and cold. Late at night, when the city was quiet, I wandered through the streets, wrapping my robes tightly around me. It often snowed. I called myself "the wandering monk in the snow."

I discovered that there were many cultural differences between Chinese and Westerners, and although I tried to adapt to

Western habits it was not always easy. I remember coming to breakfast for the first time at a Westerner's apartment. There was bread, milk, and margarine on the table, and that was all. I asked, "How come there is nothing to eat?" "This is breakfast," one of my disciples replied. "Why do you say there is nothing to eat?" We had a good laugh over that.

When my clothes tore, I mended them myself. My disciples began to take their torn clothes to me.

"You can mend them yourself," I said.

"Americans don't mend clothes," a disciple replied. "We just buy new ones."

"You are a monastic now," I said. "You must adapt and learn to mend your clothes, especially the monastic clothes, which are hard to find."

I tried to teach them how, but they would leave me their clothes anyway. "You seem to like doing it," they said.

"You have to learn how to do it yourselves," I told them.

They eventually learned. Sometimes it took some patience to teach Western disciples.

I have been fortunate to receive the help of both the very wealthy and the very poor in America. My own monastic community wasn't always as helpful. During my wandering, I often asked if I could stay at Dharma centers. The abbots would tell me, "You are such a great bodhisattva. My monastery is too small for you." If I slept in a monk's bed, where would he sleep? If I didn't, would I sleep on the floor, on the sofa, or in a chair? If the abbots could not give me comfortable accommodations, this would subject them to the risk of being criticized by me or others.

The abbots also resisted me because they were all foreigners, trying hard to survive themselves. They were worried about keeping their own place in the American Dharma community. If I spent time at their monastery, I could pose a threat to their position. Sometimes monks would come into a monastery from the outside, stay for a while, and then lead a revolt by recruiting their own followers to chase away the original abbot.

This can happen when the followers come to realize that their original teacher is not very good compared to the new one. In some cases, there's nothing wrong with the original teacher, but when the followers come into contact with a new teacher, they change and no longer want to support the original teacher. Back in China, in the golden age of Chan during the Tang dynasty (618–907 C.E.), the monasteries were large and everyone was welcome. The masters were confident and established and did not worry about a new monk taking over. Now, there are more small monasteries, especially in the United States; individuals run them, and they are not part of a large organization. So teachers do not have much security.

I empathized with these monks, and I did not insist on staying with them. They were ordinary monastics and shared the worries of laypeople. It was normal for them to have such a mentality. Not every monastic is free from self-centeredness.

I came to realize that I needed to start my own Chan center. My sangha, or community of students, had been loyal to me throughout my period of homelessness, but I knew my wandering could not go on forever. We needed our own place.

We found an apartment in Woodside, Queens, for $350 a month. I had only $700, enough to cover the first month's rent and the deposit. I told C. T. Shen that I didn't have the money to continue paying the rent, and he took care of it, graciously as always.

When we moved in, the apartment was empty. Not even a

Buddha statue. Master Haolin had a spare statue and he gave it to me. I picked up three boards on the street and made a table from them to set up an altar.

That was a happy day, when I made the first altar for the first Buddha statue in the first monastery of my own. A Chinese grocer gave us flowers and fruit, and we placed these on the altar. Then we started picking up furniture in the street. There were chairs we picked up that we still use at the Chan Center. We found forks, spoons, and other utensils, but no chopsticks.

I went to a Chinese practitioner's house and told him that we had an apartment and needed furniture. He gave me a table. I am sitting at this same table, working on this book right now.

Since we did not have money to buy food, the owner of the building, who was Thai, gave me vegetables from his garden. We would go to markets at night to pick up discarded vegetables: yams, potatoes, and cabbages that were ugly-looking but still good. We did the same with bread, picking through the garbage of bakeries.

I thought to myself that the United States is such a wonderful place—everywhere we could pick up useful things for free! My sangha were mostly poor students. They were very wonderful. We went out together to comb the streets. During this unsettled period, while I was looking for a place to establish my own sangha, my small group of students continued to practice with me. About twenty-five of us met in a large loft in Greenwich Village in lower Manhattan, which belonged to one of the students. We would gather there on Saturday mornings. We meditated, and I gave lectures and conducted personal interviews in the host's bedroom. This group was the nucleus of the people who helped me establish the first Chan Meditation Center, publish the *Chan Newsletter* and *Chan Magazine,* and start Dharma Drum Publications.

As the sangha grew, and with support from generous donors, we were able to put a down payment on a small building on Corona Avenue in Elmhurst, Queens, which had previously been a factory of some kind. C. T. Shen generously offered a significant part of this down payment. He told me the money was a loan. Later, when I tried to repay the money, Shen would not hear of it. "I was afraid that you would not accept it if I did not say it was a loan," he said. "Just write me a donation receipt."

I have always been grateful to C. T. Shen for his support, which remained steadfast even when it seemed everyone else in the Buddhist Federation shunned me. People like him are very rare. He was not selfish. He did not expect absolute loyalty; he continued to support me even after I left the temple. He treated me well from beginning to end.

As time went on, my sangha expanded; my students were still mostly Westerners, but gradually there were more Chinese. I picked the Corona Avenue location because it was cheap. A large proportion of the early Western members were college students, but the later Chinese members of the sangha turned out to be the ones with money.

The building on Corona Avenue used to be a factory with heavy machine presses. When we moved in, the entire place was a mess, with machine oil all over the ground floor. We didn't have money to pay a contractor for professional cleaning, so sangha members cleaned, painted, and did carpentry. Every day, especially on weekends, people showed up to work, and many contributed materials, such as paint, tiles, signs, and so on. After nearly six weeks of all-out effort, the building gradually began to look as though it would in fact become a meditation center.

Prior to the completion of the building we had already taken the steps to create a corporate umbrella under which the meditation center would operate. It was called the Chung-Hwa Buddhist Cultural Center in honor of Dongchu's organization of the same name in Taiwan.

At last, we were set up in our new building, my organization was stable, and I was able to offer regular meditation classes and retreats. I began to refine my technique of instruction and make it my own.

The teaching of Chan practice has a long history. The early period of Chinese Chan emphasized cultivation of samadhi, or making the mind still and silent. Practitioners lived away from society and practiced alone, in caves or mountain huts.

In the time of the fourth patriarch, Dayi Daoxin (580–651), group practice began, with large Chan organizations of up to five hundred people; followers no longer practiced in isolation. In the time of the sixth patriarch, Huineng (638–713) changed the method of practice yet again. He attained enlightenment when he heard the words from the *Diamond Sutra*: "Without abiding give rise to mind." After Huineng, Chan practice became very flexible. His method was known as the "three no's": no-thought, no-form, and no-abiding. If the mind can realize the three no's, the practitioner has "attained" enlightenment. From that time on, Chan teachers told their students that if they can practice the attitude of three no's all the time, then there is no need to learn complicated theories or methods of practice. Often Chan masters would give no real instruction other than scolding students not to get drowsy or lazy. "Death is right in front of you," they might say, chastising their disciples.

"Life is impermanent. How can you be drowsy and waste your time?"

Later, the Song dynasty master Dahui, who was an adherent of Tang dynasty master Linji, created the method of *huatou*, in which practitioners would meditate on seemingly absurd questions such as "What is *wu* (nothing)?" or "What is your original face?" or simply "*Wu?*" By focusing on such a question to the exclusion of all other thoughts, the practitioner's mind becomes more open to realizing the three no's.

At the same time, the Caodong sect espoused the method of Silent Illumination, in which you become very clear and bring full awareness to whatever you are doing—working, walking—with no self-centered attachments. The Linji school became the more influential of the two schools, and Silent Illumination fell into disrepute because Master Dahui believed it was not a proper Chan practice. Dahui, who was a proponent of the *huatou* method, did not truly understand Hongzhi's teaching of Silent Illumination. He thought Silent Illumination involved making the mind like a dark cave. Even now that I have helped to revive Master Hongzhi's Silent Illumination, there are still people in the Linji sect who think that it is misguided Chan. Actually, Silent Illumination is very similar to Vipassana and Zhiguan of Tiantai school, which is one of the reasons that my Silent Illumination retreat has proven to be very popular, drawing people who are interested in those traditions.

I teach both the *huatou* and Silent Illumination methods and have received transmission from both the Linji (Japanese Rinzai) and Caodong (Japanese Soto) lines. I don't see one as superior to another, and I have done my best to revive the practice of Silent Illumination according to the principles laid down by Master Hongzhi.

Disciples often stayed in Chan Halls for years. Some, after

hearing one sentence, let go of self-centered attachments. Some even attained enlightenment in Chan Halls. But the experiences of enlightenment mostly happened outside the Chan Hall, when a follower heard a sound, or saw something, that provoked a very strong reaction and led to enlightenment.

I took a different approach to teaching Chan in the West, adapting it to the lives of my followers, laypeople who could only stay in retreat for a few days. I disagreed with previous Chan teachings; I didn't think that it was possible to ask them to attain the three no's right away. I first taught them to count their breath, a method from my teachers in Japan, which is also used in Theravada Buddhism as well as in the Chinese Tiantai school, although even there it was rarely used.

In the United States, I divided the process of training the mind in the three no's into several stages: first the concentrated mind, then the unified mind, and finally no-mind. Obtaining the concentrated mind requires the cultivation of samadhi, keeping the mind fixed on one point. But I don't teach people to actually enter samadhi. I teach them that when their thoughts no longer fluctuate, then they have achieved a concentrated mind.

The next stage, the unified mind, seeks the unification of mind and body. You no longer feel that your body is a burden. You are very comfortable, with no itching or pain. Your body feels like a ball of cotton, a weightless mass with air flowing freely through it. Then you don't feel your body's existence at all as your mind and body and surroundings unify. There is no longer the sense of subject and object between you and what surrounds you. You become unified with the universe, without a sense of time, space, or limits.

In the final stage, no-mind, you no longer see the body, mind, and environment as the self. You can still be clearly aware of the mind, body, and environment, but there is no sense of the self in it. There is a story from Chan history about a student who asked, "In the state of no-mind, when myriad phenomena are manifest in front of you, what do you do?" The teacher replied, "Red is not white, blue is not black, but none has anything to do with you." That is to say, you can handle myriad phenomena, but the subjective self does not relate to these matters as subjects and objects. That is the mind of no-abiding. You do what you need to do, with a mind of compassion and wisdom, not a mind of self-centeredness. This last stage is very difficult to communicate. People without enlightenment will not be able to understand what it is to operate from the mind of no-abiding.

My approach is different from the approach used in China's Chan Halls. In Chinese Chan, there is no exercise other than periods of fast walking to break up longer periods of still, silent sitting meditation. I have combined in my teaching this Chinese technique of fast walking with the Theravada practice of slow walking. I also use yoga from India and Taiji and massage from China in my teaching. Westerners seem to like and respond well to this variety and the mix of stillness and motion.

I also teach my students to do prostrations, a method that has been so central to my own practice since my early days on Wolf Mountain. How many prostrations have I done in my life? It is impossible to say. The repetition of ritually lowering oneself in a series of prescribed steps until one's face is on the floor and then returning, in a series of ritualized movements, to a standing position is extremely powerful, although it's something that Westerners may have trouble with, at least at first. Some of my students have felt it to be a form of abasement, or, as one prostrates in front of a Buddha statue, a kind of idolatry.

The concept of getting rid of karmic obstructions through prostrations may strike many Westerners as impossibly esoteric, so I focus on the practical benefits of prostrating, which have to do with calming the mind. I teach people who have trouble calming down to do prostrations slowly, to fully experience the bodily movements. After doing prostrations in this manner, their bodies relax and calm down, making the space for the mind to do the same.

Recitation, or prayer, is another element of the Chan practice that I teach. The power of prayer cannot be explained by psychology or science. When we pray, we generate power. In Buddhism, we say the relationship between the person who prays and the object of prayer is like the relationship between a bell and the person who rings the bell, or a mirror and the person standing in front of the mirror. The bell won't ring without someone to ring it. The mirror does not make a reflection without someone standing in front of it. The being—the object of prayer—can only have power if people have faith in it. It's the same as in Christianity. You are saved only if you have faith. On this level, the faith in Buddhism is no different from that in Western religion. Faith is what gives prayer its power.

On another level, Chan practice generates mental power. For example, when a mother thinks about her child all the time, the child may begin to think that he should write or call her. He senses her need even though he didn't hear from her directly. This kind of mental power is universal; it happens in the East and the West. And that's just the power of one person. Consider what can happen when a thousand people recite the Great Compassion Dharani together; the power generated may create a substantial reaction, ripening causes and conditions until change occurs.

People may come together to pray for money to buy a piece of land for a monastery, for example (which actually happened in Taiwan when we were trying to find funds to purchase the land for Dharma Drum Mountain, our monastery, and Buddhist University there). It is not as if the Bodhisattva Guanyin gave those people the will to buy that land. It's the power of the mind that praying to the Guanyin generates that leads to the result, although the causes and conditions need to be ripe for the result to occur, no matter how many people come together to pray.

Chan does not encourage individuals to use recitation to ask for specific results. When Chan masters ask for something, it's not just for themselves; it's for everyone. For example, if there is a terrible drought, with the land all cracked and dried up, local officials may ask a monk to ask for rain. There are many examples when a Chan master asked for rain, and rain came. Westerners think that is outright superstition. I agree that it is indeed possible that such occurrences are pure coincidence; that when you pray for rain and rain comes, well, it was simply time for it to rain, with or without the prayer.

Still, the nature of what I do and teach cannot be explained by psychology or science. Enlightenment in Chan cannot be manufactured in a laboratory or measured by a machine. Enlightenment can only be known by direct experience, just as the warmth of a cup of tea can only be understood by the person drinking it.

I have explained some of the ways in which I guide my students. At the heart of my teaching is the idea that can be described as conditioned co-arising—everything that arises and disappears has its reasons. We are aware of some of the reasons and unaware of others. Everything that happens has a reason for happening. If we don't understand the reasons, that's because of our own limitations.

It's important to understand that causes and conditions are the most important part of the Dharma. If you understand this, you will not give up, nor will you insist on what can't be achieved,

or be jealous of others, or upset with yourself. When you encounter obstacles, you must cultivate conditions to improve your
chances of success. Even though some people practice a long
time and do not achieve enlightenment, they still find the practice very useful and full of joy.

I teach my students not to worry about enlightenment, especially since it is impossible to fully understand the causes and conditions that lead to it. I have taught Chan since 1976. Some of my
students have been practicing since before they met me and still
have not experienced enlightenment. But they don't give up.
They understand that causes and conditions are mysterious.
They don't get disappointed, or overexcited, or full of pride.

It was during these years teaching in Queens that I made
the transition from Chan practitioner to Chan master. Chan
masters are not trained, and not all monastics become Chan
masters. Chan masters must meet several criteria. They must
have seen their true Buddha-nature. They must have a good understanding of the Dharma and the ability to explain it clearly.
They must be able to communicate well, to truly reach and move
others. And they must have a place to teach.

I did not become a Chan master until I was fifty. Before that
time, I was still searching. I had not developed my own teaching
style and identity as a leader. Once I became a Chan master, I
had to cope with the burden of power, what it meant to have that
level of authority. Throughout the history of Chan, Chan masters
have known that power is merely a worldly thing, to be handled
responsibly. Some masters have indulged in power because their
practice was not good enough, and they let themselves forget
their role and responsibilities.

But most widely recognized Chan masters have known how
to handle fame and power, in some cases by renouncing them!

In a canonical story from the Song dynasty, a Chan master re-tired when he was still in his prime. One of his disciples, a high-level official, missed him and set out to find him. The official searched for him at a monastery that he'd heard was very good. He asked one of the monks if there were any great practitioners there.

The monk replied, "No, we are all ordinary people here. We eat when we eat, we sleep when we sleep."

"Is there anyone who is enlightened?" the official asked.

"Those who say that they are enlightened must not be en-lightened," the monk said. "Enlightenment is a personal matter."

Later on, the official saw a monk in the dining hall, serving meals to others, who looked familiar. The official could not think of how he recognized this person, and he asked the monk in charge, "I think I know this person from somewhere. What's his name?"

"This person has no name," the administrative monk said. "He has lived here for over a year, working in the kitchen and fertilizing the garden."

"Do you think he is a great monk?" the official asked.

"Don't talk nonsense," was the reply. "We have no great monks here."

This official went to talk to the serving monk, whom he thought he recognized, after the meal was over. "Do I know you from somewhere else?" the official asked.

The monk answered, "I should not lie, but neither should I tell the truth. You may have known him, but I don't know him." And the monk walked off to do his work.

It was indeed the same abbot who had been the official's master. After retiring from his abbot position, he moved on to do ordinary tasks. Why did he do that? He had no attachment to the power he had had in his former position.

18

Chan in the Hills

There is a long tradition of retreats in Chan. In mainland China, both the Caodong and Linji schools would devote three months in the winter and three months in the summer to retreats, during which they would close the monastery to outsiders and spend long periods of time meditating and in silence. Laypeople rarely attended retreats, although it wasn't because they were not allowed. In China's agrarian society, they were simply too busy with work to have time or be able to afford to retire to monasteries for a protracted period of time. If they wanted to deepen their practice, they could become monastics.

Also, it was generally the case in China that traditional Chan Halls were too small to accommodate laypeople. The Chan Hall was used for both practice and sleeping. In the front was a platform for sitting meditation. Blankets were stored in the back, and that's where everybody slept at night. The Dharma Hall was used for lectures on the rules for living a monastic life or admonitions to practice hard. Very rarely were there actually lectures on the Dharma.

All this has changed. Now, laypeople participate avidly in retreats. As my sangha in Queens continued to grow, our retreats ran to overflowing and we were bursting at the seams. By the mid-nineties the second Chan Center on Corona Avenue was too small to accommodate the growing numbers, so we decided to establish a more spacious retreat center outside of Queens, preferably in a rural area.

Fortunately, the growth of the sangha here was augmented by the expatriate Chinese community in the New York area, a number of whom had contributed to the development of the Queens center. As I will discuss a little further along, my organization in Taiwan was growing by leaps and bounds, and so it was possible to consider purchasing property and building projects.

In 1995, after much searching, we found a wonderful place for a retreat center in Pine Bush, New York. This was originally a private estate, which later became a summer camp for the Young Women's Christian Association. When we looked at the property, it had already been vacated by the YWCA, and many of the buildings were in a state of disrepair. But it was a beautiful site, with its own lake and walking trails, and isolated. And best of all, in addition to a main house and a dining hall, there was a large meeting hall on a small hill, which would be perfect for holding retreats.

It was about two hours away from New York City, with hills rising up at the southern end of the Shawangunk Ridge, woods of maple, oak, and beech, rolling fields, a small lake, and populated by many animals, including birds, woodchucks, deer, and black bears. It was a lovely pastoral place, within easy striking distance from the city, but there were problems. The town of Pine Bush was concerned that, being a religious organization, we would not pay property tax. So we told the officials that we were willing to contribute money to the town. Also, our prospective neighbors saw that we were Chinese and Buddhist, and more problems arose. They thought that we were perhaps a cult that would engage in strange rites and nefarious goings-on. We politely educated them to the peaceful (and quiet!) nature of our purpose, and they finally relented. Once we finally made the purchase, we were overjoyed, even though the property's buildings had poor insulation, insufficient heat, and were overrun by rodents. That didn't deter us from conducting our first winter retreat in what used to be the recreation hall.

My students seemed to benefit greatly from the retreats in our new Pine Bush property, but for some of them these retreats were a struggle. One student, a very intelligent man who remembered everything I taught, word for word, would periodically stop coming to class. I discovered that he became violent to his wife and used addictive drugs.

From time to time he would return for classes or retreats, and I would ask him why he had disappeared.

"I found your teaching so useful that I didn't feel I needed to come anymore," he replied.

"Then why are you here now?" I asked.

"I'm like a car," he said. "After you drive a car for a while, you need to take it to the garage to be repaired."

His mind did calm down, especially after retreats, and he would stop taking drugs; then he would disappear and relapse. His behavior gave me quite a bit of grief. Every time he returned, I tried talking to him, but I didn't know how to help him.

If he had stayed with me, he would not have had these problems. When he was practicing he was fine. When he didn't practice, he was not. When he returned after an absence, he was very unstable in the Chan Hall and suffered a great deal, but the practice still helped him. Eventually he never came back.

Some students suffered from pride and ambition. A student once asked me, "Are you the best teacher in this world?"

"I am not," I said.

"Who is?" he asked.

"I don't know," I said. "Maybe I am the best teacher for you now."

"Since you are not confident that you are the best teacher," he said, "I will go look for the best teacher."

A couple years later, he returned to tell me: "There seems to be no such thing as the best teacher in this world. Sometimes people told me about a great teacher, and then when I went to his classes I didn't think he was all that good."

Another student became upset that I would not help him find a place to go on solitary retreat for six years, as I had done. I told him that he was not ready to practice without the guidance of a teacher, and, in any case, it was not up to me to find him a place to go on solitary retreat. "No one found a place for my retreat," I told him. "I looked for it myself." He became quite upset that I wouldn't encourage him or help him find a place for solitary retreat, so he left our community.

Several people came to practice with me after studying with different teachers from different Buddhist sects. They left these teachers because they didn't find them or their organizations good enough. At first, they were very faithful disciples, even while holding to some of the ideas they had learned from their previous places of practice. But eventually I, also, did not live up to their ideals. They became critical and wanted me to change. They even demanded that I chase away some of my other students. I couldn't change myself as a teacher, or change our organization to fit their ideals.

These people left. We did not become enemies, and I was

not disheartened to see them go. They simply wanted to fulfill their own ideals, and when I no longer fit into that quest, they went searching elsewhere. They still learned from me and contributed to the organization. It's good when they come. It's also good when they leave. There is nothing unhappy about it. everything is impermanent in this world.

Another issue we became aware of in the 1980s was the financial and sex scandals in some of the Eastern-based religious groups in the United States. This was covered widely in the media. Most of my students were very confident that our organization didn't have these problems, but some students from other organizations came to see if we did. For a time this caused some suspicion, but no one found any problems.

I felt very peaceful about the matter. Sex and money are the two red lights in my life. I am always very careful about these two issues. I treat everyone with compassion and wisdom, not emotion.

Westerners are very passionate, though, so at times when I treat them nicely, they respond with emotion. But I am insulated. I do not conduct electricity. Even if they treat me with emotion, there will not be a connection. In the West, shaking hands and hugging are very common. I judge whether it's appropriate to shake hands, and sometimes I refuse. I don't hug. I will say that I made an exception once, when a follower of mine was leaving the community. American women like to hug, but I find it necessary to decline. Once, when I was not prepared, a woman tried to hug me and succeeded. After that, I was prepared and prevented her from doing it again.

Another factor that kept interpersonal problems from plaguing us is that my disciples don't live together in a community. After the retreats, they go home. It's very clear that we are together for practice, and that's all. If we lived in a community together full-time, maybe there would be problems with relationships.

As for money, I do not lend money to people, mainly because I don't have any personal money, although I donate money in the name of the Chan Center. I also do not borrow money. If we needed money for buying property, we borrowed from the bank. Otherwise, we are funded with donations. These policies have prevented money conflicts.

I also try to ward off conflicts over politics. In America, there are often protests against the government and antiwar demonstrations. I know that Vietnamese Buddhist organizations protested against the Vietnam War in the 1970s. However, I trust Shakyamuni Buddha, who paid attention to politics, but did not get involved. Some of my students, however, have pressed me and our organization to take a stand on political issues. They point to the Catholic Church, which openly expresses its political views, and the fact that the Pope is influential in political affairs. But the Pope couldn't stop wars from breaking out, nor could he mobilize all Catholics in the world to protest one war or another. My position is that it's better for religious organizations not to get involved in politics. My students struggled with my position at first, but they have come to accept it.

One of the reasons our Chan Center has not had many problems is that I have excellent disciples. Guo Yuan Fa Shi has been with me the longest, more than eighteen years. Our relationship is master and disciple. Wherever I go, he goes with me. He has been the head monk of Chan Center and the Dharma Drum Retreat Center. Now he is the head of the Chan Hall at Dharma Drum Mountain. He helps me conduct retreats and travels with me around the world. I would say we are like father and son, but fathers and sons get into fights and we don't.

He is grateful to me for my teaching, and I am grateful to him for his help. This is the normal relationship between master and disciple. I treat him as a student, friend, and teacher.

I always remember what Dongchu said about the relationship between a master and his disciple, that it is 30 percent teacher-student, 70 percent fellow Dharma practitioners. I can't just treat my disciples as disciples all the time. I also learn from their thinking and experiences. We are master and disciple, and we are also good friends.

I have taken up where Dongchu left off. Once he told me: "The relationship between a master and disciple is like that of father and son, like teacher and student, but it is also a friendship. The master may guide, criticize, and correct, but the disciple must be responsible for his own practice. The master cannot worry over his disciple like a mother. The master just leads the disciple onto the Path; the disciple must walk the Path himself or herself."

Sometimes, problems occur when a disciple asks his or her master for special treatment. Longtime disciples tend to get more benefits simply because they have been around longer, not because I treat them better. I treat all my disciples equally, and that, I like to think, is at least one of the reasons that their number has multiplied over these last twenty-five or so years—the final third of my life—after I finally decided to become a teacher and a leader in my own right.

My health has always been poor, but I have tried to live my life in these last years with vigor. Whenever I am needed, I go, do the project, then collapse from exhaustion. I need to rest until the next project needs me. My doctor told me that I would die soon without resting more. But whenever there was work, I felt that since there was not much time left, I should use it well to do work to help others. I need to work while I still can.

19

Drum Beats East

Once the Retreat Center at Pine Bush was well established, my thoughts turned to the possibilities for expansion of Dharma Drum Mountain in Taiwan. Over the years, I had been going back and forth to Taiwan to take care of Nongchan Monastery. I wanted to establish a Buddhist study institute there, so I began spending longer periods of time in Taibei.

At first, some of the neighbors near the monastery objected to its expansion. We were able to move forward, however. Later, when we started plans for DDM, which would attach a Buddhist University and research center to the monastery—a major construction project—there were local contractors who wanted to get the contract, although they were not experienced or skilled enough to manage a project of this scope. We awarded the job to contractors who subcontracted the project out, and we no longer needed to deal with these problems.

Because we own many properties throughout Taiwan, some of them quite extensive, we must contend with the perception that the organization is very wealthy. We are often asked for donations of money and land. We try to explain that the donations we receive are meant only for our educational projects, not to be given away no matter how worthy the cause. We give back to the community with activities and classes that are ways to contribute to the welfare of local people. This kind of outreach helps ease the tensions between Dharma Drum and the local communities in which it is embedded.

I have found that we need to maintain relationships with all spheres of society: the local community, politicians from all parties, business leaders, artists, and farmers. We have followers from all these spheres, although most of our supporters are ordinary people. We don't favor one kind of person over another, or one political party over another. We don't take this approach for financial reasons. Thousands of Taiwan's elite participate in our retreats, but I don't ask them for donations. My goal is for them to use the method and concept of Chan practice to benefit their work and their organizations. That is the contribution of Dharma Drum Mountain to society. That is our duty.

I train my monastics to ask for support from many people. If we asked for support from just a few, we would only build connections with a few. If we ask for donations from many people, we build a wide web of affinity.

Our efforts have made Dharma Drum Mountain one of the four largest Buddhist organizations in Taiwan. The largest is Ciji (commonly known as Tzu-chi), the second largest is Foguang Shan (Buddha's Light Mountain). Then there is us, DDM, and Zhongtai Shan (Chung-tai Mountain). These four organizations are often called the four mountains in Taiwanese Buddhism, but they do not oppose one another. Rather, we interact. The founder of Zhongtai Mountain, Master Weijue, and I had the same master, Lingyuan. Master Xingyun, the founder of Buddha's Light, was a student of Master Dongchu, so we are also Dharma brothers and very good friends. Master Zhengyan was a student of Master Yinshun, who was a student of Taixu. My late master Dongchu was the Dharma brother of Master Yinshun, so we are part of the same lineage.

Each organization has unique characteristics. Zhongtai emphasizes Chan practice, without the idea of spreading Buddhism in the world through community outreach. Buddha's Light has monasteries on five continents, with followers everywhere, and it is active in sangha education and outreach through its own publishing house and television channel. Ciji has no monastery, though they have monastics, and their work focuses on disaster relief, medical services, and education.

Dharma Drum Mountain has also done a great deal of charity and disaster relief work, but the organization has distinguished itself through its commitment to Buddhist scholarship through our university and our graduate institute. We are also committed to spreading the method and concepts of Chan.

We promote what we call "environmental protection" in several ways. We protect our daily living environment by keeping the buildings and surroundings simple and tidy, and we promote practical, clean living both at DDM and in the homes of our followers. We protect our social environment through proper etiquette; our followers dress neatly, speak to each other in a soft, wise, and compassionate manner, and act with respect and gratitude, without coming into conflict with others. We protect the natural environment by not wasting resources.

Finally, we protect our spiritual environment. Our followers are taught to use the concepts and methods of Chan to help themselves when they feel vexed or disturbed, instead of putting themselves in opposition to their environment. Chan helps you open your mind, accept every situation, serve everyone, and use compassion and wisdom to handle whatever arises.

Our hope is that the practices of Chan will create a Pure Land on earth, a place free from vexation. The Chan concept of Pure Land is somewhat different from the Pure Land of Japanese Buddhism, which has to do with reciting the name of Amitabha Buddha (Amida in Japanese, Amituofo in Chinese) in hopes of being reborn in the Western Paradise, a spiritual realm of bliss and harmony. By contrast, the Chan Pure Land to which DDM aspires is achievable here and now—it is primarily a state of mind.

We use the concepts and methods of Chan to help people improve not just the quality of their daily life, but to help them obtain a mind of wisdom and compassion and lessen disturbances and ignorance. Although we still live in the ordinary world, we are not affected by what goes on and do not fall prey to feelings of suffering, anger, jealousy, opposition, and frustration. There will still be earthquakes, wars, and floods, but we will use compassion to deal with these difficult events. I have many disciples who have experienced a lessening of their vexations and an increase in their wisdom and compassion—a transformation of how they experience the world. That is why they continue to study with me.

Dharma Drum Mountain now has more than five thousand volunteers, teaching Chan and doing charitable work. There are more than two hundred monastics as well, a small number given the size of our organization. This is due to the fact that we only started training monastics relatively recently. Each year, their number grows.

My commitments in Taiwan have meant that Chan has not

become as well-known in the United States as Zen and Tibetan Buddhism. My students in the United States could not have strong solidarity with me because I was always going back to Taiwan. I would have a group of students for three months and then I would be gone. My students would have no one to study Chan with after I left, as the other Chinese monks in America stayed within the Chinese community and did not know English.

When I would return to the United States after half a year, my English would be rusty, and that made it difficult to attract new students. My most committed Western students began studying with me during my first two years in the United States, the longest period I was there continuously.

If I stayed in the United States for a decade without a long absence, I would probably have many more Western students. My good friend Thich Nhat Hahn did so, and he is very popular in the United States. He arrived in the West from Vietnam in 1974, just a year before I did. He has also spread his teachings through his poetry and other writings. His prose is much more beautiful than mine, and very few Chan masters are as prolific as he is.

With the success of our organization has come responsibility and also enmity. There is a Chinese saying, "When the tree is large, it catches wind." We are the object of envy, and because we are large and command substantial resources, there are people who want to take advantage of us. But we make a practice of treating everyone with compassion, even those who are jealous of us or opportunistic.

20

Full Circle

I think of myself as a citizen of the world. As a religious teacher and monk, I do not belong to a certain people or nation. I am like a cloud, drifting from place to place. I have traveled all over the globe, and the earth feels very small to me. Each place is connected to the others.

There is an old Chinese saying: "When leaves fall from the tree, they will return to their roots." That is to say, when people get old, they want to return to their birthplace. And so, some years ago, I made the journey to Jiangsu, the place of my birth.

My parents were already dead. My mother passed away when she was still in her fifties, and my father died when he was in his eighties. They were alone in their later years. Like almost everyone else in China at that time, their children had to struggle to survive in impoverished conditions. I know that if I had stayed on the mainland, I would have had to leave our little village and the hardscrabble life of subsistence farming to become a monk or go elsewhere to make a living. And even if I had not left home or become a monk—if, by some wild stretch of imagination, I had found a way to survive close to the mother and father who had raised me, I can't imagine that I would have been much help to them. I have observed both in the East and the West that children nowadays very rarely take care of their parents. Parents, however, often need to take care of their children, even late in life. At least I didn't need my parents to take care of me.

I stood in Jiangsu over my parents' graves. My brother told me that when my father was dying, he had no idea where I was because once I left the mainland I had no way to contact them. My father thought that I had died in the chaos of war. As I gazed at the graves where my parents' bones were buried, the thought of my father on his deathbed—not knowing if his youngest son was alive—made me weep. My tears were tears of helplessness and gratitude. I felt helpless that I was not able to be with my parents when they passed away, and I was grateful for all they had done for me.

The sadness I felt at my parents' graves has passed. I am a monk, and monastics must leave worldly emotions behind. Worldly emotions include relationships with parents, friends, and women. I don't become entangled in relationships: that would inevitably lead to suffering. I still have compassion for people, which is an emotional connection. But if I had worldly relationships, I would not be able to be a good monk. There would be problems.

In recent years, I have begun to slow down. I still get up every day, meditate, and do the morning service in the Buddha Hall. I may go to the Chan Hall afterward. After breakfast, I read the newspaper, or my secretary summarizes the online news for me. I still teach classes, but no longer train disciples personally. Experienced disciples train them.

I don't spend much time on administrative matters; all I

have to do is sign off on important documents, or give guidance on how to handle situations that arise. I often turn to my students for help; many of them are experts in their fields and know how to deal with problems.

Much of my time is spent receiving visitors. Some are important or famous, others are not. I see people no matter who they are. My visitors seek guidance from me; they want a few words of Dharma.

Now that I am old, I need time to rest in the afternoon. When I was younger, I worked sixteen-hour days without resting. There was no time to rest; the organization was young and so much needed to be done. I could push myself, but now I need a slower pace. There are times when I need to return to my place in Taibei to rest with my attendant and my secretary accompanying me.

I try to keep myself open to new experiences and people so I can continue to learn and grow. I am particularly fond of the old Chinese proverb "When the tide rises, the boats also rise."

It is important for me to continue to develop, even in my old age. I think of the story of Dahui's enlightenment. His master, Yuanwu, wanted to test Dahui's realization, and gave Dahui the only copy of a book that he, Yuanwu, had written. Dahui responded by burning the book.

"Why did you burn my book?" Yuanwu asked.

"It's such a rare opportunity that a hunter can kill a fat hog," Dahui replied.

The master was very pleased to hear this. "I wasn't so fat before," he said. "It seems that I have gained weight."

This master was glad to see his book go up in flames because that would prevent him from continuing to teach what he already knew, what was familiar to him, what he had already worked out in his own mind. So you see, very talented students force their teachers to learn more. I have continued to learn from my students. They help me deepen my practice.

Time has passed so quickly. I am hardly aware of the shifts from adolescence to middle age to old age. I'm sure that my inner world now is different from my inner world thirty years ago, but I can't really explain how they are different. Has my experience of Chan practice deepened? I don't know. The only difference I feel between now and thirty years ago is that I once had more energy and my body was stronger.

There have been other changes, too, but they are subtle. Now that I am old, more of what I'm thinking stays inside me. I am more contained. The things I want to express do not always need to manifest outwardly; they dissolve in my mind. For example, when I used to see students being lazy during meditation, I would hit them with the incense board to arouse their diligence. Now when I see students being lazy, I just watch them to see if they will discover their lack of diligence by themselves. If they don't, I use Dharma lectures to remind them of what they need to do. Perhaps this is because my body is not as strong, and my mental reactions are not as strong either.

My reactions to women, fame, and money are different as well. When I was young, I would see women and recognize that they were women, even though I knew I would uphold the precepts and not touch them. Now, to me, women are no different from men; people are people; we are all human beings. I don't even have to affirm that according to the precepts of a monk, I should not touch women. Now, there is simply no difference between my way of responding to women and men.

I have said that the two red lights in my life were women and money. Now the two red lights are no longer there, because I no longer need to constrain or stop myself. I needed the two red lights before because I was still training my mind to avoid temptation. But now deliberate training is no longer needed; it has become natural to me. I am old, and I am used to it. In my mind, gold is no different from dust. They are both just material things.

Looking back, I can say that I never planned for my life to turn out a certain way. When I was young, before I became a monk, I did not know what I wanted to do. Even after I became a monk, I didn't know whether I wanted the monastic life, or what it meant. I had heard of a monastery that was looking for fresh faces and, as I had no other prospects, I went there and became a monk.

If that hadn't happened, I would have kept on being a child in my poor village, no different from my siblings and the other kids I played with. Instead, my experiences at Wolf Mountain gave me the general direction of my life—to share the Dharma with others. It was something that took hold inside, even when I was in the army.

When I returned to the monastic life, the Nationalist government and all the high-level officials were Christian. Buddhism was dismissed in Taiwanese society, and I wanted to improve its status. That was one of the reasons I went on solitary retreat. No schools accepted monks at the time, but I wanted to deepen my practice, to read, write, and educate myself so that I could stand the best chance of having an impact on society. That is also why I went to university in Japan. Causes and conditions made that possible. I had published books and had friends who studied at Rissho University, and they helped me get in, despite my never finishing high school.

My life has progressed through one set of causes and conditions leading to another. If C. T. Shen had not invited me to come to the Temple of Great Enlightenment in the Bronx, I would not have developed my method of teaching Chan practice by adapting Buddhist traditions for Western students. If I had not developed this method, I would not have been able to teach Chan. For that matter, if my master had not passed away, I would not have returned to Taiwan, and Chan practice would not have spread as it has from my efforts at Dharma Drum Mountain and its affiliates.

I believe I have been very fortunate in my life. There is one principle that has remained constant: I never allow myself to experience feelings of satisfaction or disappointment. When things are going well, I don't let myself feel content. When I encounter obstacles or failure, I don't despair. I find ways to keep going. When I encounter a dead end, I turn around and find another way to proceed. I keep moving. If I stop, there is no hope.

That push for movement—to continue no matter what the obstacles and difficulties are and not give up—has been the guiding force in my life. I am old now, close to my death, but I still see a road ahead of me. I do not think I am done.

I am not attached to what I have accomplished in the past. People have honored me, but I can't eat honors. When the Mahachulalongkornrajavidyalaya University in Thailand gave me an honorary degree, the rector said that I didn't need the honor— it was their honor for me to accept the degree. But I felt ashamed; I didn't feel there was any honor that I could possibly deserve. I feel myself to be a very ordinary person. My accomplishments are not mine; they are a result of causes and conditions which I did not avoid but, instead, willingly took on because I wanted to alleviate suffering and help people.

My attitude of not taking personal credit for my position and refusing to toot my own horn has, at times, been frustrating for my followers. For example, a number of years ago, Taiwan's then president, Lee Denghui, invited me to his home to teach him meditation. When my Taiwanese disciples found out about this, they became very excited, thinking that Master Sheng Yen is now the teacher of the president. They felt we must spread the news. I said we must not.

"Shifu is now like the sun at noon, at its peak," they said in their effort to urge me to tell everyone.

"You must not think that," I said. "I am just a monk. The president heard that I can teach meditation, and meditation is good for health and mind, so he asked me to teach him. What is so special about that?"

When Lee ran for reelection, he wanted the Buddhist vote, so he told people Master Sheng Yen was his teacher. When I learned of his claim, I said, "I only taught him for two hours. I am not his teacher. The president said that to acknowledge that he is interested in meditation."

The day after he was elected, Lee came to see me. I gave him a scroll inscribed with these words: "With compassion there is no enemy, with wisdom there is no vexation." He hung the scroll in his office. When people found out about my gift, they got very excited again. "These are not my words," I said. "These are the words of Buddhadharma. The president hung them in his office because he is wise. His actions have nothing to do with me."

I have been asked whether there is anything in my life that I regret. I have experiences where I did embarrassing things. I still do plenty of embarrassing things. But there is nothing I regret. When I make a mistake, I repent, accept responsibility, and keep going.

I have been most embarrassed when I have not been able to accept my failures. When the officials at the Chinese Culture University closed the Graduate Institute of Buddhist Studies, I should have refrained from commenting. But I petitioned the university's president to keep the institute's doors open.

"Master," the president said to me, "you are a monk. You should not be attached to success or failure." I was abashed. Here I was a monk, and this layperson was teaching me Dharma! It was a great experience, though. I learned a good lesson.

I believe that I have been able to help people through my life, and I have been able to spread the Dharma. I still think of myself as a wandering monk in the snow. I go where I am needed. I have established centers for Chan practice and study in Taiwan as well as in the U.S.A. and Europe, and Dharma Drum Mountain has thousands of members. It has been good to take up the story of my life and set it down in English. I hope it will be of some use. Now it is time to let go.

Epilogue

I am now over seventy-seven years old. Because the course of my life was a mini-version of the recent history experienced by Chinese people and society, the history in this book may be well-known to Western readers yet feel unfamiliar. My motivation for writing an English autobiography was to connect with Western readers. The content of this book is different from my two autobiographies and the biography of me that have been published in Chinese. A small part of it overlapped the Chinese books, but most of this book is new.

The book is very much my memory of my life. It is impressionistic, not a perfect record. But because of the work done by the interviewers, Rebecca Li and Kenneth Wapner, I was able to recount my experiences in some detail. For me, the personal details of my life do not seem worth writing about. But for readers, they may be interesting. That is why the interviewers came back for more interviews over and over. So I want to thank them. I would also like to thank Doubleday for publishing this book.

My blessings and thanks to all my readers.

Editor's Note

~ ~ ~ ~ ~ ~

This book came together over a number of years and through the efforts of a number of people. After working with George Crane on *Bones of the Master* (Bantam, 2000), I felt that Chan Buddhism, Chinese Zen, was underappreciated in the West. I approached Sheng Yen, perhaps the best-known Chan teacher in the West, and asked if he would be willing to work together to produce his autobiography in English. He agreed, and Trace Murphy, Sheng Yen's editor at Doubleday, expressed enthusiasm for the project.

At least one biography and two autobiographies of Sheng Yen already existed in Chinese. I commissioned Bill Porter (Red Pine), the brilliant translator and author, to translate some of this material and used this, as well as interviews with Sheng Yen himself, to construct an outline of his life, which formed the spine of this book. Writers Paul Smart, Tad Wise, and my wife, Corinne Mol, helped in the early stage of this process.

After I had the basic outline of Sheng Yen's life, I interviewed him and submitted written questions to him to which he responded in Chinese. Sheng Yen spent many hours answering my questions and hosted me in Taiwan so I could get a sense of his organization there and travel to some of the places that appear in the book.

Sheng Yen's answers to my questions were transcribed and translated, and I edited them to form the book you have in your hands. The writer Lisa Phillips was an enormous help in the final stages of bringing the manuscript into form, and Ernie Heau, Sheng Yen's longtime editor and disciple, gave the final manuscript a good hard read; his comments improved the book immeasurably.

I have saved the person who did the lion's share of the work on *Footprints in the Snow* for last. Rebecca Li, a professor of sociology and disciple of Sheng Yen, who is fluent in both Chinese and English, spent countless hours interviewing Sheng Yen in Chinese and feeding me English text. She also read through Sheng Yen's Chinese material and added information where needed. She did all this out of the goodness of her heart and her belief in the value of the work. Thank her if you like the book, and blame me if you don't.

Kenneth Wapner
April 1, 2008